Memories of a GREY-HAIRED OLD BRUMMIE

Ronski

First published in Great Britain as a softback original in 2020

Copyright © Ronski

The moral right of this author has been asserted.

All rights reserved.

No part of this publication may be reproduced, stored in a retrieval system, or transmitted, in any form or by any means, without the prior permission in writing of the publisher, nor be otherwise circulated in any form of binding or cover other than that in which it is published and without a similar condition including this condition being imposed on the subsequent purchaser.

Typeset in Palatino

Editing, design, typesetting and publishing by UK Book Publishing
www.ukbookpublishing.com

ISBN: 978-1-913179-42-7

chapter 1

A wet Sunday morning at the end of July and I'm at a loss to know what to do...so I've decided to start a trip into the crevices of my grey matter and churn out what I find there.

The reader may wonder what this old fool, at 74 years of age, has to say that has any significance at all to his or her life or anyone else's for that matter. Well probably nothing, but at least we'll give it a go.

As you get older and look back at your life you realise that, as I once wrote in large capitals on my garage wall, WE ARE ALL A PRODUCT OF OUR GENETICS AND PAST AND PRESENT ENVIRONMENT. What I failed to add in order not to be too harsh on my neighbours at that time (or maybe I did) was AND NOTHING ELSE!

You see the neighbours were generally God-fearing country people who were welded inextricably to tradition and village life, and this intolerable intrusion that I had made into their lives by this graphic outburst being now compounded with the inference that God did not exist would surely have been too much, and my end of terrace cottage would have probably been burnt to the ground!

This is a rewind back to the mid-1980s but much went on before this time. A time that is now only vaguely remembered and, regretfully, so much is now lost in the decaying crevices...why didn't I write stuff down then...silly man.

The very distant past finds me living with my parents in a council house in a suburb of Birmingham only four miles from the city centre yet within a stone's throw of farmyards and fields...What are we doing to this planet? It's getting more like Venus every day! Anyway the Second World War had not long ended...you know the one after the one that was the War to end all Wars and my very earliest recollections are of a cold winter with the smell from a small paraffin heater filling my nostrils. I slept in a corner of my parents' bedroom, the other two bedrooms being occupied by much older siblings. The larger back bedroom was occupied by my elderly twin bothers, soon to be conscripted into the army and the smaller back bedroom by the eldest of my siblings, my sister, soon to escape my father by getting married!

Time passed and it wasn't too long before my parents and I were the only occupants of our 25 year old three bedroom house that my parents had lived in from the time of its construction. My father was a skilled carpenter of average build and size with a very large chip on his shoulder, having been too young for the First World War and too old for the second, and having gone through the depression and the means test with three young children to support; all of which had helped to embitter him against the rest of society ...a trait which I have unfortunately inherited. To his credit, despite a minor wobble in the 50s he, at least, remained loyal to Mom until the day she died, despite many eruptions of angst. Another plus with my father was that, strangely, he always showed a great deal of respect towards the rest of the animal kingdom... another trait that I, fortunately, have inherited.

My mother, a small dumpy woman was, probably like many other mothers, an "angel". Long suffering, kind, tolerant, loving and the complete opposite to my father. A father whose only escape from reality was visits to illegal (at the time) bookmakers to place his bets ... yet another dubious trait that I have inherited...you see where the GENETICS keeps coming in.

The memories of my pre-teenage years are fragmentary; I remember my father in the early fifties winning 2nd dividend on the football pools (Birmingham City scoring in the final moments of their match letting him down for the major prize). This was a windfall that enabled us to be the first family up our road to own a television and led to a cramped living room full of neighbours watching the "Matthews Final" of 1953 on our little 12 inch Echo. About that time I remember being dressed up by my Mom and sister to celebrate the Queen's Coronation. I seemed to recall the outfit was supposed to represent some sort of joker, being made up of a grey silky material with loads of playing cards sewn all over it...don't ask! It rained anyway and it got totally soaked.

Mornings at that time were invariably cold and I usually shivered my way down the stairs to watch Mom cleaning out the spent ash from under the grate before she prepared my breakfast of bread and milk. Occasionally I would be up in time to see my father go off to work, with the smell of Sloan's Liniment disappearing out of the door with him. My primary school was directly opposite our house, so leaving the sound of the Home Service behind, I would cross our deserted side road to get some education. I recall the smell of horse manure often entered my nose whilst crossing that road because the horse pulling the early morning milk float had made his own delivery. A delivery that after school I often had to scoop up for Father's roses.

Christmases were always a special time with uncles coming to visit with their presents. Often I was given half a crown by both Uncle Norman and Uncle Harold but what I actually did with the money I cannot recall. John, one of my twin elder brothers, once gave me a set of six Dinky racing cars in their colourful livery ...Maserati, Ferrari, B.M.W., Lotus etc... If only I had kept them! I was also given one year a double-barrelled pop gun that shot corks some considerable distance; it would certainly not be allowed today.

Of course, our Christmas toys then were but few and as a result were highly prized and usually lasted throughout the whole of the following year and beyond; unlike today where houses are full of different plastic toys that children do not look after and the sheer variety of which lead to children having the attention span of bemused lemmings!

John, the younger of my twin brothers by a few minutes, would often take me, at this time, with his girlfriend Pat to watch football matches. One week we would go and watch Aston Villa play and the next week West Bromwich Albion. We once watched W.B.A. beat Manchester City 9-2 and I suddenly became a lifelong "Baggies" fan.

The most significant event at this time, however, was that I became a "grammar grub". Yes, miraculously, I had passed the 11+ exam. My memories of taking the exam itself are pretty sketchy but I do recall there was a bus journey through snow-covered streets to King Edwards Grammar School in Aston and some memory of being ushered into a classroom full of Dickensian type school desks...and that's about as much as I can recall. At the age of ten it was all very nerve-racking so how I scribbled enough correct answers to pass amazes me. Anyway the upshot of it all was that I ended up with my 3rd choice school...that of Handsworth Grammar School. The fact that it was nearly five miles and two buses away from where I lived did not seem to matter too much. At this time, as a consequence of my "elevated status" I soon lost most of my council estate friends, including my friend from up the road and his elder sister who I had been playing doctors and nurses with for years!

The grammar school that was to educate me over the next five years was certainly Victorian in its nature, one that Wackford Squeers would, truly, have been proud of! The Headmaster was the Reverend J.J. Walton, a man that time had forgot, and who certainly believed in "spare the rod...spoil the child"...as I found to my cost on a couple of occasions during my internment there. Each morning, having crossed half of the inner suburbs of Birmingham on smoke-filled buses, I had to face the ritual of morning assembly with the whole panoply of teaching staff assembled on stage in front of me. A terrifying bunch with just one female amongst them; Miss Keeling was an elderly spinster-type woman who was supposedly an ex-Magistrate and was quite capable, like the rest of them, of reducing me to tears on more than one occasion. "Holy Joe" (Walton) was the headmaster's nickname and he or his deputy, a rotund Churchillian-type character, whose name quite escapes me, presided over these early morning "get-togethers". The usual hymns were belted out including, of course, Jerusalem, a song that seemed to be sung practically every day, and then, usually, we would finish with the school song, namely "The Old Bridge Trust" (words by the Reverend J. J. Walton). So many experiences, both pleasant and unpleasant, occurred during my time at Handsworth Grammar School that I need a short break now to try and recall the most significant of them!

Chapter 2

Of course, what I failed to tell you about Grammar Schools was that, on arrival, you are attached to what is called a "house". Mine was one of eight and was called Hart. This was general practice for all Grammar Schools at that time; the idea being, I suppose, to link you with a group of other pupils in some sort of common bond against the other "houses"; promoting comradeship and encouraging competition throughout your years at the school. You often played all of the major sports against the other "houses" and sometimes even more cerebral games such as chess. Every month or so there would be a house meeting in which the progress up or down the house league table was discussed. The other interesting feature of our grammar school was that of "streaming". This was a method of winkling out the brightest of the boys from the dross and enabling them to miss a whole academic year...so you went from the 1st year to "remove" and then to "shell" and finally ended up in the 5th year, one year ahead of the majority of the pupils...I was dross, although I did progress from 1D to 5Q amongst the "also rans".

There was also a cadet force for those more interested in military stuff and I was roped in for a period of time; the main memory of this episode was going to a camp near Aldershot and being addressed at a huge rally by Field Marshall Montgomery, although squatting on the grass about 200 yards away from him made it impossible to hear what he was saying...but his gestures and mannerisms made his identity unmistakeable (unless, of course, it was his double)! He was a strict disciplinarian and the school discipline was administered, besides the teachers and a "cane-happy" headmaster (ouch! that hurt 10 times!) by a group of schoolboys known as prefects. Each "house" had its own prefect to keep their particular flock in order and then, of course, there was the "head prefect". He was, without doubt, a total and complete oik and patrolled the corridors, swagger stick in hand, administering punishments where he saw fit and snitching to the headmaster or his deputy when any boy showed any resistance to his authority. Not surprisingly he was also "head" cadet which made your life as a pretend soldier almost impossible...so I didn't last that long in the cadet force as you might expect.

Wednesday afternoons were allocated to sport and after lunch we had to make our own way to our sports field; a distance of some two miles, which I had to walk, along with some other fellow pupils who also could not afford the bus fare. Every month the sports field was exchanged for the swimming baths and since the baths were just down the road from the school they were much easier to get to than those "remote" playing fields. Remembering to take your swimming gear to school on those monthly swim days was always quite difficult and one day, I recall, I completely forgot and knowing detention awaited me for not remembering, I was totally down during an art class. The art teacher, a Mr Yeats, sensed my anxiety and offered to take me home in his open-top sports car during lunch break in order to get my swimming stuff. I must admit I felt a bit uncomfortable at the time about the whole idea but the thought of an after school detention for forgetting my kit swayed me into accepting his offer. He drove like a maniac, braking hard at one stage to avoid hitting a lamppost; in hindsight I suspect the whole idea was to perpetuate among the boys through my inevitable storytelling of the journey, an image of an edgy free-going spirit amidst the dour discipline of the old school. Mr Yeats was one of the few teachers that seemed to buck the trend in a teaching staff full of establishment lackeys...he often wore a cravat instead of the usual collar and tie to signify his unorthodoxy. Most of the other teachers were bulk standard including some with rather dubious habits. A Mr Derby or was it Derbyshire was one of these worrying creatures; he took us for French and every lesson he would stand in front of class with one foot on a chair and the opposite hand in his pocket continually fiddling around with his tackle! No wonder French was one of my weaker subjects.

Around the time of my early years at grammar school two health related events occurred in my life; one was to be a fairly short term blip, the other had fairly profound long-term effects. The short term event was that one Saturday night I was rushed to hospital with appendicitis and after a week there recovering, I spent the next six weeks at home, away from school, with a post operational infection. The more significant long term event, although I did not recognise it at the time, was that whilst mucking about in the toilets with another boy...no not that way...I was spun around into the concrete corner post of a toilet door and had my two front teeth partially knocked out. A subsequent visit to a dentist with my mother resulted in a decision being made for me to have false teeth fitted rather than the more expensive crowns. At the time this seemed no big thing but later when I became more seriously interested in the opposite sex, I became more self-conscious about having false teeth leading to a total lack of confidence when trying to "pull".

Anyway, back to the story...the thing about grammar schools then was that you were continually being assessed...yes the dreaded school reports. Fortunately, or possibly unfortunately, I have managed to keep all of my old school reports from over sixty years ago and here are some of the little gems that appeared in them. But, first, I must comment on the detail that each subject teacher made on every report; all comments were hand written in ink, they gave you a % mark, a grade and then a personal assessment of your progress or otherwise during that particular term. It must have taken them hours of overtime to have completed all reports for all pupils at the end of each of the three term year! Do teachers still do that anymore?

In my first year, at Easter, my form master described me as a "good steady worker, keen and helpful" but by the end of that academic year in July this had been reduced to " a good steady worker"...presumably I had no longer become "keen" or "helpful"! In the second year at Christmas my German teacher wrote "Good. Handicapped by a communicative disposition" and by Easter the same teacher wrote "inaccurate but keen". My form position at this time had slipped down to 31 out of 36 and for the only time throughout my time at grammar school Holy Joe himself wrote in RED ink on my report "Not good enough"! Fortunately, by the end of that year I had risen to the dizzy heights of 8th out of 34 (what happened to the two missing pupils I cannot recall but there is a vague memory of an epileptic boy in the class who died in his bath by electrocution from a submerged mains radio...although, of course, that may just have been schoolboy gossip). In the third year, once again, by Easter my form position had sunk to 31 out of 33 and my form master wrote "there is no doubt at all that he has been slacking" and that Easter term report is littered with fairly derogatory remarks from most of my teachers... I'm not sure what happens to me in the spring. Anyway, by the end of that year, once again I had made a dramatic recovery, finishing 14th out of the 33 in my class. My maths teacher writing "A very able boy capable of even better than this but spoiled by his lack of self control"...how true. In the fourth year it is all middle of the road stuff, ending in my usual end of the year rally to improve from 20th to 10th. The most frequently used words by my teachers throughout this particular year were erratic and inconsistent. My final year at Handsworth Grammar ended up with me remaining roughly mid-stream throughout the year with the word "satisfactory" being the most used to describe my work and with that year culminating in 5 out of 8 successful "O" levels (history, geography, maths, physics and chemistry). Strangely, despite my fairly average "O" level results, the school seemed keen on me continuing my studies despite my decision to leave at the end of the fifth year (and not to continue in the sixth form), by offering me a place in their science laboratories as a Lab Assistant; although I can't recall any pay for the work being discussed. Clearly my parents were against this idea as it was about time, at 16, I got out into the world and started contributing to the household finances in some small way...remembering that my father left school at 13 years of age to earn money. There are times throughout one's life where critical decisions are made that profoundly affect the course of your life and this was one of mine, although there were some further down the line that were even more significant...but that's for later.

Chapter 3

My final recollection of H.G.S. was of some vague and fragmented memory of returning on a Speech Day in the early part of 1962 in order to receive my "O" level certificate. I recall the place seemed totally different to the place I had left only nine months earlier. I'm grasping to remember my feelings at that time but unworldly, detached, sad, remote even, may well be the best way to describe them. It was not the same place at all.

Presumably, I had to take a day off work to go to the Speech Day, and that was from my first regular paid employment at the Dunlop Rubber Co. (although I now suddenly recall having had a part-time job in the school summer holidays at a butchers shop in Perry Barr... how revolting)! My first job at this company was to measure the characteristics of cut up tyres...in hindsight I cannot possibly see what useful purpose this served! Yet there was a "laboratory" full of people that dissected tyres randomly chosen from the production line in order to take detailed measurements of its construction...Why? We took measurements concerning the tyre's beads, its sidewall thickness, the mid-crown shoulder's thickness, the shoulder thickness, the crown thickness...Why? I can only assume that it was some sort of quality control assessment...but even if a particular tyre proved to have been constructed correctly it was no guarantee that the guy that made this tyre was going to make his next one to the same standard. I suppose it made work for the working man to do. We dissected and scrutinised the construction of all types of tyres including aircraft tyres, earthmover tyres, assorted car and motorcycle tyres and even ordinary cycle tyres. The costs involved with the whole exercise must have been considerable, particularly with the very expensive large earthmovers. I remember looking out across one of the main railway lines into Birmingham from the company's main tyre storeroom and seeing the green grass of Birmingham Racecourse. The storeroom is now an office block and Birmingham Racecourse is now a housing estate surrounded by an elevated motorway! Anyway, my time in that part of the company was quite brief but it did encompass the Christmas party. Liquor was surreptitiously introduced into the proceedings and I got pleasantly pissed and introduced to a girl "outsider" who was a friend of one of the workers there. As I disappeared out into the cold night air with my arm around her shoulder, I remember quite distinctly one of the older workers shouting, "you'll be alright there"! So it proved. It was not long before she had inadvertently dropped one of her earrings down her cleavage …and it all kicked off from there. I will not go into detail here, but she seemed to enjoy her journey "down south"!

From the main Dunlop complex I was transferred to Dunlop Research Centre on the Kingsbury Road and what a transformation that proved to be. Out of the grime and smells of tyre production into academia and research into the production of synthetic latexes. I was now mixing with a load of post-grads, posh boys and generally more switched-on people. Life seemed richer somehow and early mornings would often start with a group of us lab technicians trying to find the answers to the day's Telegraph cryptic crossword. Once we got "warmed up" with that, the normal business of the day would start. This involved the measuring of the properties of various latexes we had produced in our pilot plant the night before or on previous earlier occasions. Before too long, because of the additional pay, I became involved with the production side of these latexes. It did involve working a 24 hour shift once or twice a week...something that would be a total no-no now; and often we had to make trips out to the chemical pound in the middle of the night to collect butadiene, styrene or the more dangerous and volatile acrylonitrile for their polymerization in the pilot plant vessels. Breathing apparatus was required when dealing with the acrylonitrile and sometimes your apparatus visor would "steam up", particularly in the cold night air, not allowing you to see what you were doing. Holding your breath without the breathing apparatus on was the only way of charging up your carrying vessel to the right level, and sometimes that sweet oniony smell of the deadly acrylonitrile would penetrate your nostrils...yuk! Of course, once charged with all the right chemical ingredients in the correct proportions, the polymerization process inside the reaction vessel would have to be monitored on a regular two-hourly basis...the conversion rate from monomer to polymer being the key criteria.

Now getting a couple of tired lab techs to stay awake at two in the morning after starting work 18 hours earlier was not always easy. We had a Dunlopillo mattress to allow one of us to sleep for a bit while the other worked, but often things didn't always work out. Quite often sleep overcame both of us on a shift and waking up with only minutes before everyone rolled in, led us to hastily take samples from the reaction vessel, quickly measure its monomer to polymer conversion rate and fill in any missing monitoring times on our paperwork with guesstimate figures!

There were even worse occurrences when I worked with one particular heavy-sleeping co-worker who continually slept during his supposedly "waking" period and led us, on one or two occasions, to being discovered "asleep on the job". After one particular episode it was discovered that polymerization in one of the reaction vessels had "run away" during the night and completely bunged up the whole of its insides with solid rubber. We were not very popular that day with our fellow technicians, who would have to spend the rest of that day stripping down the vessel and clearing it all out. Management were not pleased either!...but they were a forgiving lot ...probably having been in the same position themselves in the past, and luckily for us the affected vessel was one of the smaller ones and not one of the very big reaction vessels that contained hundreds of gallons of "stuff".

At this time pubs were quite a big thing in my life and with my fellow technicians John M. and John O. we often spent our free time in the evenings crawling around most of our nearby establishments. John O. was a year older than me, very clever but slightly eccentric; he purchased an old enormous open-topped green Rolls Royce car that he used to come to work in. It occupied two parking spaces when parked much to the annoyance of management and the delight of us workers. John M. was my age and on the small side. He was obsessed with motor racing and I recall going with him to a motor racing track and being disturbed by the noise, the smells and the boring processions around the track by these wretched machines. It was an uncharacteristically sociable time for me, talking and mixing with a lot of very clever people from diverse backgrounds and learning a lot about human nature and what makes us tick. The pubs were smoke-filled places at this time and to my shame I often contributed to the atmosphere by indulging myself. I, once, single-handedly organized a day out trip to London for many of my fellow workers at Dunlop Research Centre. I collected the money from interested personnel throughout the centre, hired a coach from a local transport company, and with a coach full of people one Saturday morning set off to the capital. I can remember very little about the whole experience but I do remember an inspection hatch in the main aisleway of the "iffy" coach continually bouncing up and down over every bump in the road and being paralytic and sick in some seedy nightclub and having to be helped back to our coach (wherever that was)! I think at the time I was trying to pull a secretary we called "the Sphinx" because of her inscrutable smile and I believe she was on the coach to see me being dragged on board...how humiliating! At some stage I did get a date with her and we went back to her parents' house along the Kingsbury Road where she showed me her pet snake (I kid you not) and after that encounter things seemed to fizzle out.

When I was not at work I would often frequent our local snooker hall with a friend from just down the road. We had a fairly loose relationship throughout my grammar school years and into adulthood. We both enjoyed a game of snooker and the large back bedroom at my parents' home had once contained a half-sized billiard table that we spent hours practising on, so we were fairly decent at potting balls. The other attraction of the snooker hall, besides being a place to secretly smoke cigarettes, was a gaming machine called Jumbo. My angel of a mother often unknowingly subbed me money to feed into the wretched device, which rarely paid out. This weakness for gaming machines once led me to frequent a cafe just up the road from where I lived, where there was a pinball machine that you could win money from; by nudging and slightly tilting the machine you sometimes made a bob or two. Anyway, at this cafe I engaged with an attractive young girl who wore thick-lensed glasses and who seemed quite keen to strike up a "friendship". In hindsight, I suspect she was probably underage but at the time it did not appear that way. We made a date to meet at one of the nearby cinemas, and when I arrived there early, surprisingly she was waiting outside. After the usual backrow stuff we walked home through an adjacent playing field where I took total advantage of her, with her full and enthusiastic consent of course. After I had done my stuff she disconcertingly said, "A bloke I know usually rolls on his back when he's about to come."...HELP! Oh yes help indeed, as a few days later my doctor diagnosed N.S.U.!

Whilst at the Research Centre my academic studies continued at night school. I went to Matthew Bolton Technical College in Birmingham to study organic chemistry. It was a two night a week job so fitting it in with my shift work was not too easy. That's probably why I moved from Dunlop Research Centre to a conventional day job at Dunlop Chemical Products on the Chester Road. Once again it was laboratory work but this time it was concerned, primarily, with exploring the use of different latexes on the back of various carpet materials but also any other applications for the stuff anyone could think of. Whilst I was there I went out with an office girl whose name totally escapes me, but I do recall sharing the most intimate of moments with her in my bedroom to the sounds of Scheherazade coming from a record I had put on my player to try and enhance the mood of the tryst.

I did not stay long at this new place of employment before an urge to try something new got the better of me and I started a new job working for a company called Tufnols in Perry Barr. This company made laminated plastics and resin-based materials. Once again it was lab work, concerned this time with the insulating properties of the stuff that was produced. Even though I was not working for Dunlops anymore, I still retained my links with their sporting club. The exact chronology of events during this period is lost in the mists of time but I do recall around this time I found myself running for a bus, jumping on the open platform at the back of the bus and panting vigorously for the next few minutes. Enough is enough, I decided, my twenty-a-day cigarette habit was about to end. Now having dabbled with indoor shooting, judo and hockey at Dunlops when I was there, I now decided to join their athletics club to recoup my fitness. So once again this exhausting run for a number 33 bus once again led me down a path that would eventually change the course of my whole life...read on!

It was decided, by me or others, that I would be tried in a two-mile event as my first competitive race for Dunlop's Athletic Club. It was against a local athletics club on a grass track in a park in Sutton Coldfield. There are eight laps of the track in this event and I was lapped ...nearly twice! Oh how unfit I really was! Towards the end of that meeting one of our sprinters had to pull out of the 100yards event with some sort of injury so to make up the numbers I was elected to run in his place. It was on an undulating grass track against five other rivals... I won by about 5 yards easing down and my fate as a sprinter for the club was secured. Of the many events I competed in for Dunlops there are three particular events that I remember fairly vividly. The first to be recalled took place in Mountain Ash, South Wales on New Year's Eve 1967 or was it 1966...can't quite remember the actual year. However, it was part of the Nos Galan sports event that takes place there annually. There is a round the houses race of about 3 miles or so and some sprints down the High Street...I entered both. Fortunately, the sprints took place first and amazingly I got through my heat against some serious rivals...and in the final I finished 3rd beating among others the world famous long jumper Lyn Davies. It all becomes a bit of a blur after that and I vaguely recall being whisked off into some sort of large crowded hall and being interviewed on TV by some Welsh commentator asking me what it was like to beat Lyn Davies...I think I coughed and spluttered a bit and blurted out some totally pap reply. The round the houses road race I took part in after was done so in a state of complete euphoria even though I finished closer to last than to first and it was only at the end of the race when the cramp started to set in did I start hurting. After that I think I recall a journey back to the locker room of a local colliery and settling down to sleep in a sleeping bag on a hard cold floor. In the morning we were treated with Welsh hospitality to a full English breakfast in the colliery canteen...and a breakfast has never tasted sweeter.

The second event to be recalled was a trip up North to the ash running track of the Pilkingtons Glass Factory. I was to run as a second string to my coach Ron Taylor (who incidentally still holds the WORLD RECORD for an over 60s athlete at 100 metres) in a 100 yards event. Ron was of Caribbean descent with a relaxed attitude to life (except on the athletics track, of course); he was constantly playing tricks and always cracking jokes. He would take his wristwatch off before a race and grease between his thighs in order to gain every advantage he could. Anyway on the Pilkington track I clocked a 10.0 secs time with Ron just ahead in 9.9 secs...my fastest ever time over 100 YARDS.

The third recollection I have was of an athletics meeting that took place in Shrewsbury in the summertime of 1967 I think; at this meeting I won several prizes including a large brown porcelain horse ... an item that was soon to disappear out of my life only to re-emerge unexpectedly nearly 40 years later!

Of course, I lied to you when I said there were three events I recall; there was a fourth and this one is the real doozy.

Chapter 4

In 1968 the Warwickshire County Championships were held at Leamington Spa and I was entered for the sprint events. I was eliminated early on in the 100 yards and only just scraped through into the final of the 220yards. This final was one of the last events of the afternoon and some of the finalists decided to leave early so I managed to get a 4th place. Paul X and his brother hung on to give me a lift home in their car and reminded me on the way that it was Marg's 21st birthday party that evening in her mom's house in Sutton Coldfield. Marg had often followed the exploits of our athletics club and often came with us on our trips to other clubs. When I arrived home I was totally knackered and lay in the warm water of our old cast iron bath knowing the time of the last bus to Sutton was fast approaching. I think Mom shouted something like "are you going or not?" as I sank below the warm bubbles of the inviting bath...it was so much a fifty-fifty decision...my athletic group knew I was not a particularly sociable person so they wouldn't be surprised if I didn't turn up; on the other hand Marg had been supportive of us for some time ...what should I do? ...oh sod it, I'll go. Out of the bath, into some dry clothes, a dab of aftershave, a sprint down the road just in time for the last bus to draw up to the stop and allow me on. This was without doubt the single most pivotal moment of my whole life.

When I arrived at the party I was hailed as some sort of conquering hero (or were they just taking the piss?...who knows). I was briefly the centre of attention which I so hated and my self-consciousness quickly kicked in; the only way out was the drinks table and after a quick couple of shorts things became a bit rosier. My induced high became even higher when I met Marg's younger sister, Joyce – she was an absolute belter. We almost made touchdown that very night and it was not long before a night in a Tamworth B&B cemented our relationship. A hasty marriage at a registry office in Sutton was followed by a reception at Joyce's house. Both my father and elder brother Dennis and his wife Margaret all refused to attend either function on the grounds that "marry in haste repent at leisure". At 23 years of age I was clearly too young to make a rational decision. The good news was that Mom, my other brother John and his wife Pat, my sister and her husband Bernard did decide to attend along with Joyce's Mom, Marg and some of our friends from the athletics club. Incidentally, Joyce and Marg had lost their father whilst they were both in their early teens... They discovered his body in an armchair and I suspect it had quite a traumatic effect on both of the girls, particularly the younger Joyce who I had just married. We honeymooned in a caravan at Burnham-on-Sea and I returned to live with Joyce, Marg and their Mom in their house in Sutton.

I lasted just three months before I returned to my own home with my tail between my legs. Living with three women was just beyond me; I simply could not cope with their ups and downs, particularly Joyce's. My idea was to get some high paid jobs over and during the approaching winter to be able to put a deposit on a house, so that I could live with Joyce on our own. It was a bleak time for me. I got a job at an injection moulding company during the day and became a barman at night. I had no contact at all with Joyce or her family, and thought that I could easily breeze back into her life in the spring with keys to our own house and all would be well...what a total plank!

The work at the injection moulding company was piecework and I worked a machine that pressed out all sorts of plastic nonsense for the car industry. Since I thought I knew something about ergonomics I laid out all the paraphernalia that I had to use in such a way that I could load my press in the minimum amount of time and therefore make more components and therefore earn more money...what a naive idiot I was. To think that a young newcomer was going to earn more money than workers that had been there for years...you must be joking! The stuff I produced, along with all the rest, had to go through quality control, so, sneakily, my stuff was more severely scrutinized than work done by the established members of the company; this resulted in 20% of my work being rejected... I suppose if you'd worked in this grimy shithole for as long as some of these guys had you deserved your rewards in the weekly pay packet. In the evenings I got a job in a local pub as a barman which was work that was always a struggle for me because of my total lack of confidence and slightly shaky hands...but I managed somehow with the thoughts of an eventual place of my own with a happy Joyce by my side. Whilst at the pub I was briefly introduced to the "Buffs"...a supposedly charitable organization but that actually turned out, in my case, to be nothing more than a drinkers' club...I soon kicked that one into touch! The tune that was continually being played on the pub jukebox at that time was "Hey Jude" by the Beatles and every time I hear it now it always "brings me down".

Spring came and by the end of March into early April I had saved enough money to make some sort of a deposit on a house, so I set forth to surprise Joyce with my well-earned wealth. I knocked on the front door and her mother answered and said "she doesn't want to see you" and closed the door in my face. I think I shouted Joyce's name and her mom replied something like "Go Away"" My thoughts went into the red zone; being rejected after all that effort made me lose the plot completely and I smashed my fist through their front door window.

Blood dripped from my hand and I stormed off down the road. After a couple of minutes a policeman walked towards me, clearly having been summoned by Joyce or her mother, but seeing the intense anger on my face he decided to walk on by. My state of mind at this time was one of anger and frustration and not knowing what to do I sought out a Marriage Guidance Counsellor; strangely the office of this woman was in the same building where I had taken my marriage vows less than a year earlier. Her advice, after getting in touch with Joyce, was that I should leave well alone and go off and start a new life elsewhere.

Chapter 5

The RAF Recruitment office in Birmingham were quite impressed with my qualifications and put me down as a potential "Ground Radar Technician".

Basic training took place at RAF Swinderby and lasted about six weeks. Our intake was about 40 strong and for some unaccountable reason the NCOs in charge decided to make me Leading Man. The main perk of this was that I had a small room of my own to sleep in whilst the rest had to share communal sleeping arrangements. One or two of my group should have been in prison rather than the Air Force but most were OK. I do recall being winched up in a glider for a fly around the airfield one weekend ...the first time I had ever been off the ground in my life. I survived the experience despite my problems with vertigo. We "passed out" after six weeks or so and I was dispatched to RAF Locking for a mechanics course in the disciplines of Communications and Radar. The only recollection I have from this particular period at RAF Locking was watching the Moon landing in the early hours of the morning in a television room full of Iranian airmen...how times have changed!

Now I cannot remember whether it was at Locking or at my first posting at RAF Cottesmore, Rutland that I received a summons from Sutton Coldfield Magistrates Court to answer a request for CHILD MAINTENANCE! On reflection I think it was certainly RAF Locking, as a possible liaison with a ginger haired girl from Wolverhampton I met on a train had to be terminated after this gob-smacking news. The ginger haired girl had been travelling down on the train to Watchet in order to work in a hotel there when I met her, and a series of letters between us followed, culminating in me possibly going down to Watchet to stay with her...but all that was no longer a goer anymore! I was a father and never knew, even the Marriage Guidance woman did not bother to tell me; shame on her...but maybe she was afraid of my reaction at that time...who knows. My vaguely sympathetic commanding officer allowed me time off to travel up to Sutton and in the courtroom I saw Joyce and her mother for what transpired to be the last time. They made their case and I made mine and in the end the authorities dismissed their appeal and I left to return to a life in the RAF.

RAF Cottesmore was situated in the northern part of the now defunct county of Rutland. When I was there the aircrafts that you were most likely to see were Canberras and the bloody noisy Vulcan. I remember very little about my time there although a four and a half mile walk from the railway station in Oakham to the camp on a cold, frosty, dark and starlit winter's night sticks in my memory. It may also have been at that camp that I saw, in their small cinema, the film "The Prime of Miss Jean Brodie". Surprisingly, this film had quite a profound effect on me at an emotional time in my life as it deals to some extent with relationships and the passage of time.

It was not too long before I returned to RAF Locking on my fitters course. This course was to last the best part of 14 months and cover everything radar. Once again my memories are fragmentary about this time in my life but there are episodes I do recall. I had continued my running whilst in the Air Force and someone somewhere decided I was good enough to represent the RAF against Cambridge University. The meeting was at a track in Cambridge and I had to make my own way there by public transport. I had to start out at 5:30 in the morning from Locking, cross the entire country by train and bus, only to finally arrive at the venue just minutes before my event was due to start. The Cambridge lads were a couple of very fast South African students and I was 2nd string to an officer, namely Don Halliday ...a Commonwealth and Olympic athlete! Not surprisingly, I was slaughtered, trailing in 10 yards or more behind the other three runners...embarrassing or what! I was never considered for the RAF again after that... I knew it was not my true running... but nobody else did!

Weekends at Locking were usually free and to relax after a week's study I used to train along the pathways of the Mendips and enjoy the views, often looking down at the small village of Locking and the nearby airport...all gone now I believe, thanks to an expanding population and the insatiable appetite of developers. Despite the discipline of the Air Force some of us in my class still considered ourselves to be "free spirits" within the system and in this time of Tariq Ali we decided to have printed up some red t-shirts with an image of a mole emerging from the ground on the front. We would wear them during off-duty hours and nobody seemed to notice our "naughtiness"...probably because they didn't get it!

After lessons during the evening one of the guys with a car often used to take us into Bristol for a pizza at an Italian restaurant there and afterwards a couple of us would go to a nearby bridge club to play a few hands against the locals, while the rest sloped off to enjoy the delights of the rest of the city.

Trips to nearby Weston-Super-Mare were always a regular occurrence and I once saw "The Move" in action at the Winter Gardens there... or was that on my mechanics course a couple of years earlier...the old grey matter can't be sure.

I finished my fitters course in April 1972 as a Junior Technician with a certificate of merit for displaying "outstanding ability" and was duly shipped off to RAF North Luffenham back in Rutland again, to work on the third line repair and maintenance of, primarily, radar equipment. I seemed to recall that there was a services language school there and I dabbled a bit in Russian for a short period. Also the diminutive Princess Margaret once paid us a visit while I was there and we all had to be spruced up for the occasion. I continued with my running, winning medals at group level and command level. I trained on the ups and downs of the nearby undulating terrain. The bottom of one of the nearby picturesque valleys that I used as a training area is now fifty feet underwater as part of one huge reservoir required to supply the never-ending appetite of our expanding population. At this time I, periodically, went home to see my parents. Sometimes I used the train and sometimes on a Honda motorcycle I had bought. (I had previously owned a small green BSA Bantam in my Dunlop Research Centre years, so I knew all about these machines). It was on one such visit to my parents in the summer of 1973, that a trip to our local small bookmaker with my retired father led to a huge winning bet. I had a combination bet involving the prediction of the first and second horses home in three races; two races at Yarmouth and one at Brighton. A horse called Father Christmas completed a seventeen and a half pence winning bet that resulted in a return of about £1,740... and you know to my eternal shame I only spent a miserly £170 on my mother...I bought her a washing machine!

Before I continue I must tell you about the RAF... It was a life of work and discipline and when I signed on the dotted line in their recruitment office in 1969 I was committed to the rules and regulations of service life, but in the RAF, at that time, there was also recreation and there was also adventure; and with a "pocket-full" of cash I was about to embark on the adventure of a lifetime.

Chapter 6

In that summer of 1973 I had volunteered and been accepted for a six month detachment to Belize in Central America. This army camp was essentially a rest and recuperation centre for personnel that had been in conflicts in various parts of the world including Northern Ireland.

About fifteen or twenty of us flew out from RAF Brize Norton in August of that year and that became my very first flight in a powered aircraft. We crossed the Atlantic and stopped off overnight at Gander in Newfoundland, Canada for refuelling. To my surprise, despite the time of year, it was cold and snow covered and my only vague recollections of the place were of a hotel bar and drinks in the evening and a continental-style breakfast in the morning; a breakfast that was to re-emerge when our plane hit some serious turbulence shortly after take-off on the next leg of our journey. I think I remember looking down on New York at some stage before our flight continued its course down the east coast of America towards our next refuelling point in the Bahamas. It was to be a short stay on these islands and as the plane hurtled down the runway to recommence our journey there was a sudden and dramatic application of brakes. The pilot informed us that he was concerned about the state of one of the engines and that we would have to stay overnight while the engine was fixed. Unfortunately, it was discovered that nearly all of the hotels were fully booked and it was only the most luxurious of the hotels on the island that could actually put us up for that night...how convenient! There were palm trees, a truly turquoise ocean and delicious food to eat...I seem to recall crab was on the menu that evening.

The following day we continued our journey and arrived in Belize in the heat of the day. The transition from a cool aircraft interior into the Belizean "sauna" was almost indescribable. The hot humid air hit you like a sledgehammer and having only experienced a temperate climate throughout my life before, it was a total shock to the system. Within minutes of my arrival there I was totally covered in sweat; a condition I stayed in throughout most of my time in Belize.

The army camp itself was situated next to the airport and about 10 miles or so from Belize City. When I was there the airfield was just a long concrete strip cut out of the jungle with very few associated buildings, nothing at all like the pictures I see of it today. It was essentially a military airfield that only sporadically dealt with the very small civilian population that was interested in (or could afford) air travel. A large wooden "hut" with a nice veranda on one side was to be the sleeping quarters for about eight of us while we were there and there were similar buildings for the rest of the Air Force contingent. The army or should I say "Pongoes" also enjoyed the same sort of accommodation. These buildings were, somewhat erratically, dotted around other parts of the camp site. "Pongo" was an endearing expression frequently used by RAF personnel to describe members of the British army... and I'm sure they had their own particularly endearing slang words to describe us as well.

The work site for the RAF was a small area about 200 metres to one side of the centre point of the airport runway. When you looked towards the runway it was quite a sandy outlook interspersed with the odd bush and outcrops of tropical vegetation; a habitat in which the friendly iguana often roamed, gulping up ants, other nasty insects and the lumps of bread thrown by benevolent airmen. On this site there were two large metal "containers"; one contained all the necessary communications equipment and radar displays that were required for the RAF Air traffic controllers to do their job; the other container, which had a rotating radar dish on top, was full of all the radar processing stuff...I spent most of my working time maintaining this kit. The only other erection on our site was a very large tent in which our personal bits and dabs were kept and where we brewed up our cups of tea and coffee. Sugar, biscuits and other tasty edibles were kept in sealed tins to protect them from marauding ants and other nasty insects, and when rolling down the tent "flaps" you always had to be aware of some lurking scorpion dropping on you. Finally, I forgot, there was, of course, a large generator on site to power all of our energy requirements.

My first excursion into Belize City was by taxi after nightfall with a couple of my RAF friends (dark always descended at about 6:30 p.m.in these parts) and as we travelled along the road I was horrified to hear the continual crunch of the taxi's wheels running over countless land crabs. In the headlights ahead you could see wave after wave of crabs crossing the road; it was totally impossible for the driver to miss these unfortunate crustaceans. Our destination in the city was to be the notorious "Big C", a serviceman's corruption of its true name, that of The Continental Hotel.

I cannot tell you my utter and complete shock as we drew up outside this building. It was a very large wooden "shack" with a pair of louvered half-doors at the front that you had to go through in order to gain access to the "hotel's" insides. Anyone who has ever seen an old western movie will be familiar with similar doors at the front of every town's drinking saloon or "watering hole"; and if I found the external appearance unsettling, the "hotel's" innards were even more jaw-dropping!

The whole of the large interior was painted black and the long dance floor that stretched out to a distant bar was illuminated with the occasional dim spot of light from the ceiling above. Along both sides of the dance floor were a number of dilapidated tables and chairs and on one side of the room behind the tables, chairs and wall there, there was a hidden corridor (which I discovered a few days later) led to the rooms above. Interspersed along the wall behind which the hidden corridor lay there were several openings at about upper torso height that did not appear to have any useful function. However, after we newcomers had bought drinks from the bar and sat down on the worse-for-wear chairs, these wall apertures suddenly sprang into life with the emergence of the faces of attractive young women of assorted ethnic pedigrees. Yes! It was a knocking shop, a house of ill-repute, a whorehouse, a brothel – and the faces that appeared in the many apertures along that wall were those of young prostitutes! Soon a jukebox in the corner of the room started to play and the young girls started to file out and sit down in nearby chairs. It was all like some strange dream that not even my most wild imaginings could have dreamt up. Some of the girls were not my cup of tea at all but two or three I found particularly attractive. There was a young girl with the most wonderful aquiline features who I got into stuttering conversation with using the best of my limited grasp of the Spanish language, and discovered she came from El Salvador of Pipil extraction and her name was Marie Ethel Juarez. I bought her a few drinks and left with my friends later that evening without availing myself of her services. On the way back to camp it became fairly clear quite quickly that a couple of the guys found the whole exercise quite off-putting and turned it all into the subject of a number of predictably tasteless jokes, but I was full of curiosity about the life of my newfound prostitute friend intermingled, I admit, with a degree of basic youthful lust.

We worked a shift system back on site and this allowed me to have time off for two or three days at a time. I quickly explored the city of Belize during the hours of daylight on one of these early rest day breaks, and found the attractive smells of the open market a complete contrast to the stinking smells issuing from the nearby river. There were a few interesting shops down the main street, but I was also interested in a means of getting hold, in readies, of some of my recently acquired gambling winnings. Fortunately, I seemed to recall, there was, surprisingly, a branch of Barclays down the High Street in this out-of-the-way part of the British Empire, and since this was my bank at that time in the UK, I suddenly had a regular source of loot. It was not long, therefore, before I succumbed and availed myself of the services of my attractive friend in the "Big C".

Around the earlier part of my time in Belize I recall an expedition into neighbouring Guatemala to visit the Mayan ruins at Tikal. This whole exercise was fraught with danger as that country still had claims on Belize. A visa was organized from the local embassy for four tourists; our occupation was declared as being "in Government Service". There was a young Pilot officer and three of us "rankers" in the group as I recall, and we travelled across Belize by jeep towards the border with Guatemala. The roads through the jungle were almost non-existent, full of dangerous dips and potholes, and the conditions were hot and very humid. I remember stopping by an inviting pool en route somewhere, to have a break and some food. There was a debate about having a dip to cool down before we continued, but the discarded remains of a spam sandwich thrown into the pool soon dismissed that idea tout suite! The sandwich was immediately attacked by a horde of large ravenous piranhas...close shave or what!

I suppose we must have crossed the border at Melchor De Mencos as it seems to have been the only possible crossing point according to a map I have recently looked at, but I remember nothing of any border checks that must have been made there. We proceeded in Guatemala to a town called Flores where we stopped, for the couple of days of our visit, in a reasonably priced pension. A map of Guatemala on one of the walls in this lodging, rather disconcertingly, showed Belize as a borderless part of the country of Guatemala. There were two things I can remember about my visit to Tikal. The first was that a bamboo hut cafe in the surrounds of the Tikal complex was run by a couple from Nottingham of all places. The second revolves around my climb to the top of the tallest temple in Tikal. The journey up to the top was over worn steps, but you were assisted in your ascent by a large chain draped over these steps so that you could, at least, grab hold of something on your way up. Getting to the top was no major problem as I did not look down, but at the small summit an acute attack of vertigo overtook me and seeing my distress a pair of French pensioners who shared the small summit with me protected my descent with their bodies...How embarrassing! Where my comrades were at this time I've no idea, but there was never any mention of the incident, so I assume, thankfully, they never witnessed it. Had they done so my life would not have been worth living.

The passage home to Belize must have been totally uneventful as I remember absolutely nothing of the journey.

The girls of the "Big C" were not allowed out of the building without payment to the owner. There was a small payment for a morning or afternoon escape but getting them out at night was pricy. I felt it was grossly out of order that some young girls in Central America, through lack of work in their own countries, were required to work as prostitutes in a foreign country and then treated like prisoners when they got there into the bargain. When I confronted the owner about the girls' lack of freedom during the day he mumbled something about having paid for their travel to Belize and that he needed to recoup his outlay in every way possible. I think the poor girls even had to pay to go out of the building in order to send some of their pitiful earnings back to their families in their respective countries.

I took my Pipil girl out during the day on several occasions and a couple of times in the evening. One evening we once went to this restaurant that was in a house raised up on stilts. The woman owner was Creole and was clearly not too happy about our being there, but it was a slack night and so she decided to stomach it for the sake of cash I suppose. Having said that, the food was OK and my enduring memory of that night was getting my ankles bitten to death by a load of ravenous mosquitoes. My ankles became swollen to twice their normal size and I was in pain for days afterwards...good job I was taking my malaria tablets on a regular basis!

When not working on a Wednesday afternoon a group of us would hire a boat and go out to the Cays for a bit of snorkelling, drinking and general relaxation. The Pipil girl came with me on at least one occasion so my mates knew what was going down. She even shared my bed back on camp one night after the camp had staged a barbecue and dance in the grounds. In order to earn some more cash she became an exotic dancer named Sulema on some Saturday nights back in the "Big C". I tried to avoid going down into town on that night but one Saturday, stoked up with a few rum and cokes from one of the nearby drinking "sheds" close to camp, a colleague and I went down into town and entered that house of ill-repute. We sat down and got even more drunk than we already were. I felt a bit embarrassed watching Sulema perform her rather amateurish exotic dance and when she had finished and started to go upstairs with some tall Pongo I blew a fuse. It was inexcusable but I attacked the soldier with a tirade of abuse and punches were thrown. We brawled across the dance floor getting close to the bar area, my mate was trying to pull me away and the friends of the Pongo were doing likewise. The confrontation was getting close to the entrance of the bar itself and the owner clearly had fears for his stock and his till so he produced a revolver from under the bar and threatened us all with the weapon. It had a sobering effect on us and we eventually dispersed in our different directions. I never engaged with my Pipil girl again despite further visits to the brothel during my time in Belize. It transpired that the Pongo involved in the fracas was a scally, which explained why, in preceding days, my faltering conversations with the Pipil girl always seemed to revolve around any knowledge I had about The Beatles and Liverpool in general.

I must apologise to any reader who has actually continued to read this stuff in that the exact chronology of events at this time in particular, and for that matter the whole of this history, might not be as precise as it should be, but I can absolutely guarantee that it is totally and completely the truth.

Anyway, to continue the tale; around this time I decided to utilise some of my free time and my cash on a solo trip to El Salvador. I managed to obtain a visa (I think) from the appropriate embassy (I would have been "in government service" of course), and flew out on one of those short-haul jets that had its entrance at the rear. On my arrival in San Salvador an accommodating taxi driver outside the airport drove me to a pension. I cannot remember anything about that place, unfortunately, but it was to be my base during my three day stay in the city. I think the taxi driver, who was rewarded generously for his services, became my means of transport throughout the whole of my time in that country. There are a few memories that stick in my mind from this visit and I shall try and recall them as accurately as I can.

Visiting the colourful shops and market stalls of San Salvador I did notice that I stood about a foot taller than most of the people there, and with my limited Spanish managed to make one or two souvenir type purchases. The thing that struck me most when dealing with the various stallholders was that their reluctance to engage with me initially turned to complete co-operation when they discovered that I was British and NOT American! I do remember, on one occasion, walking down some side road or other, camera in hand, and spotting a rather attractive church to photograph; and raising my camera to eyelevel was immediately yelled at by some rifle toting soldier. What I had failed to notice was that there was a military pound full of tanks and other military vehicles adjacent to the church. I tried to explain that I was only interested in a picture of the church, but he was having none of it and moved me on at gunpoint. When dropping me off at my lodgings on one of the evenings my taxi driver friend started talking about "mujeres" and he said he could introduce me to a nice young girl later that night. He duly arrived later and took me to the single roomed dwelling where this girl lived. She was small and of average looks but seemed quite welcoming and invited me in . Her mother was in, but I saw no father, and there were two other younger siblings there, who were both watching an old T.V. in the corner of the room. I took the girl out for a few drinks and she told me she was a secretary during the day and I felt she seemed genuine enough. After an evening of small talk, in broken English and poor Spanish, and too much to drink by both of us, we ended up in a motel room full of mirrors performing various acts of affection towards one another. One of my days in El Salvador was engaged in a trip to a place called "Los Chorros", an out-of-town beauty spot. It was truly a beautiful place with waterfalls and attractive pools and, when I was there, the most startling array of large coloured butterflies I have ever seen. I notice now, via the internet, that the place has become highly commercialized with underwater lighting in the pools, wooden walkways and stepping stones across the more inaccessible parts of the site. My journey to and from this site was by local bus, totally full with passengers and their goods...how I managed it all, goodness only knows. Whilst I was in the country I thought it wise to get in touch with our embassy and as a result I got, surprisingly, invited to an evening meal with the charge d'affaires in his large bungalow type place in a swanky area known as Escalon. I was very nervous at meal time, especially as the food included peas... not good for a shaky hand! Anyway the charge d'affaires, whose name escapes me, had said he was going to return to the UK via Belize in three weeks' time, and since he was a keen diver, could I organise some charged up air tanks for his use when he passed through, so he could go out to the Cays for some underwater exploring. I, somewhat recklessly, agreed to the request.

Back in Belize I told my Flight Sergeant about the charge d'affaires' request and we awaited a telegram from him as to when he was going to arrive. I think it was about this time that some sort of function was going down in Belmopan, and this newly emerging capital city was inland by quite some way, and don't ask me how, I managed to get a lift, to and from the place, in an army helicopter. It was a small two-man Sioux helicopter and as the pilot skimmed the machine over the jungle canopy I defied my vertigo by riding only halfway inside the perspex bubble, with the leg outside standing on one of the helicopter's landing runners. I must have been well drunk at the time but it was so exhilarating! Belmopan at that time was a "building site" with very few buildings but it did now, at least, have a fire station, I seem to recall. This story had the destination as being Belmopan but despite having definitely visited the place at some stage, my helicopter ride, which absolutely did take place in the manner described, may well have been to some other function occurring deep in the jungle.

The awaited telegram from El Salvador finally arrived and told us the diplomat's arrival was to be the following day. Blind panic ensued as nobody knew anyone who had scuba divers' tanks or the means by which to charge them up...Help! After a chase around from place to place in an attempt to find someone somewhere who could help us out with our requirements, we chanced on someone who put us in the direction of a young American guy on one of the Cays who hired out diving gear. It transpired that he was having problems with his compressor but he said he would try his hardest to get a couple of tanks charged up for us. We got the stuff we needed from our American friend on the very morning of the charge d'affaires' arrival and hastily hired a boat for that same afternoon so that the diplomat could go on his dive. Several of us, including one of our officers and my fight sergeant, went out or the boat with him and despite fairly choppy weather the day was a success, helped, of course, with the aid of plenty of drink.

You would have thought after my earlier experiences in the "Continental Hotel" I would have learnt my lesson about fraternising with the girls there. Oh no! Another attractive girl caught my eye. Her name was Sandra Murillo and she hailed from Spanish Honduras. Her features were totally different to those of my Pipil girl; her face was much more rounded and she was probably Mestizo with a bit of Afro thrown in. She had long black hair and was particularly stunning... at least to me. Going "arriba" with her, as with her predecessor, was really no place to go. Upstairs was fairly disgusting; there were several small rooms to either side of a main corridor and their barred window interiors consisted of a bed, a few personal effects and not much else. Halfway down the corridor there was one toilet room with a primitive cold shower; this room was always filthy and had to serve all of the occupants of the establishment. The girls also had to wash their own clothes in this revolting room. My distaste for these premises caused me to pay for Sandra's release from the place on several occasions. Whilst out, we were often treated to black looks from the locals who rightly guessed her profession, but we were too busy exploring language differences between us to care too much. Sandra was a much "friendlier" girl than the Pipil girl.

I would hate to think that you, the reader, thought my time in Belize was just one long hedonistic experience...it was not. The time spent on these out of hours experiences were but a small fraction of my time in the tropics; RAF work being the most time consuming by far. Running was still in my blood and an early morning run around the airfield was a regular pursuit; often a troop of kit-carrying pongos were also spotted running in their more disciplined formation, alongside their noisy drill sergeant. On one very wet tropical morning, amidst the deluge, I spotted a mass of flies ahead of me hovering just above the surface of the road. When I got closer the huge shape lying in the middle of the road proved to be a run-over boa constrictor. It must have been twelve to fifteen feet long and the girth of this snake must have been at least four feet in circumference...enormous! Clearly he must have spent every night swallowing many of the huge number of continually croaking frogs in the area. The running route around the airfield included the approach road to the camp and passed the Belikin beer factory. This factory was only a few hundred yards away from the entrance of the camp and every time you asked for a beer or a cerveza anywhere in Belize you always got a Belikin. Incidentally, anytime you could find an excuse to go into the factory, it was such a blessed relief from the oppressive humidity and heat of the outside, as the air inside was always chilled. I can't remember whether the camp meals were prepared and served in a solid building or in a huge marquee, but these hot army-provided meals were always given to you from a servery absolutely covered in cockroaches. Going out in the evening to one of the nearby drinking "sheds" for a beer you would have to pass the guard room where condoms from a large box on the desk were always freely available to those who needed them. Rumour had it that some disgruntled Pongos on reluctant guard duty occasionally got their revenge by sticking pins into the wretched things...I never availed myself of their use. The drinking places close to the camp were indeed nothing more than wooden shacks with a crude bar to prop yourself up against (when required). They seemed to only serve Belikin or rum and coke from a clapped-out old fridge and if you needed a piss then the dark wooden toilet shack close-by always seemed to contain the discarded skins of large tarantulas....if they didn't move you were usually alright. During the day, on one occasion, I did see an army bus, loaded with the girls from the "Big C" inside, arrive on camp, and was told it was so that the army doctor could make sure none of the troops were going to catch anything really evil from them. It was, I was also told, a fairly regular occurrence.

New year's Eve was spent with a couple of my mates in a much more respectable hotel in the centre of Belize City. It was here that I was introduced to the "Club Sandwich" for the first time and the place where I got totally smashed, probably reminiscing in my mind about times gone by in some far distant land. The hazy memory recalls a small dance area where limbo dancers performed, and later, lying on my back on the roof of a moored boat, on the river somewhere, gazing up at a sky completely full of stars. There was a gentle swaying of the boat and the arms of Morpheus stretched out to embrace me!

It was in the early hours that the grab handles on the roof of this boat only just came to my rescue when the wake of a large passing vessel disrupted my slumber. Despite the grab handles' aid I think I still managed to get my feet wet and the sudden awakening sobered me up enough to get a taxi and return to base.

Whilst in Belize I'm not sure how many weeks it took me before I realized that the large buzzing "insects" flying around any available flower were in fact very small colourful hummingbirds, and I can only assume that my lack of observation was due to the myriad of other distractions there were in this strange tropical world; and yet another distraction lay ahead of me now in the form of a trip to Mexico City. Now, once again the chronology of events in Belize is unclear to my faltering old brain, but my feelings are that this journey took place towards the end of my tour of duty in the country.

I think the same party that went to Tikal earlier were involved in this excursion. Visas were acquired from the Mexican embassy for four "tourists" to visit far-off Mexico City, some nine hundred plus miles away from our base in Belize. Who came up with the idea of this trip, and why, I've no idea, but one morning we set off on some rickety old bus destined for Chetumal on the Belize/ Mexico border on the first leg of our epic expedition. This particular bus ride proved quite eventful because of a confrontation between the driver of the bus and an old Dutch couple. The dispute concerned the Dutchman's refusal to extinguish a newly lit cigar as requested to do so by the driver. The Dutchman maintained that it was a very expensive cigar and it would be an outrage to put it out. The driver was having none of it and told him if he did not put it out, he would throw him and his wife off the bus. After a few minutes of stalemate on the now stationary bus, and with the rest of the passengers getting a tad restless, the smoking Dutchman eventually decided to take his wife and their luggage off the bus, and they were now left stranded by the side of a dusty and deserted road in the middle of the jungle while the rest of us disappeared off into the distance. At Chetumal we and the rest of the passengers on alighting from the bus were amazed to find a smoking Dutchman and his wife already there!...How?...when hardly a vehicle passed us...spooky or what!

The trip by Greyhound bus from Chetumal up to Mexico City was interesting in the variety of climatic zones that we passed through. We started off in a hot and humid tropical region, passed through a more temperate area where pine trees grew, and ended up on the dry, almost desert-like, plateau on which Mexico City was built. The route was less direct than today's traveller would use, and our journey encompassed going through the towns of Villahermosa, Veracruz and Xalapa. Since a lot of the trip took place during the night, I missed a lot of the scenery and only remember glimpses of the towns and villages that we drove through. I recall Veracruz as being quite industrialized with lots of stuff associated with petroleum production there. This contrasted vividly with my memories of the villages around, and the town of, Xalapa. This area seemed, in my memory at least, an idyllic temperate pine-covered paradise...I'm sure the reality of today probably does no longer match up to what is lodged in my grey crevices! I think it was in this area of our journey that our bus was stopped by three heavily armed policemen. They checked all the passengers' paperwork and our particular documentation seemed to puzzle them somewhat, but they eventually allowed the bus to continue. My faltering Spanish inflicted on one of the fellow passengers managed to discover that the police were after some renegade "banditos". I do remember that the bus driver tried to make up for lost time by driving like an absolute maniac along some very twisty and dangerous mountain roads; at one stage he drove almost up the exhaust pipe of a labouring petrol tanker ...but we survived.

Mexico City seemed to be devoid of any tall buildings, as I recall, and seemed to cover a vast area. The hotel that we stayed at was just three storeys high. Our rooms there were on the upper floor of the hotel and I can remember running up two flights of stairs there and being completely out of breath at the top. I had totally failed to fully understand the effects that Mexico City's elevation above sea level could have on the human body!

During one occasion while we were there we decided to visit the site of a well-known Aztec ruin within the city itself and we made use of the immaculately kept underground rail system for the journey to and from the site. On the way back it was rush hour on the underground and we were squashed like sardines in the train compartment. Our group all stood head and shoulders above the indigenous population and one of my fellow Junior Technician mates, a ginger-haired Scots lad, who was six foot three, really exaggerated this height difference. I can remember his smirking face to this day as three very small and very attractive girls brushed up against his body...he was clearly in the most pleasantest of places...until that is, in the street above our desired underground stop, he discovered all his pockets had been completely emptied! Yes someone had taken the lot...his wallet, his passport, his visa...all gone. A hasty visit to the British Embassy ensued, in order to explain to them his new circumstances. I think they must have managed to organise some temporary paperwork with the Mexican authorities for him, because our visit seemed to continue without a hitch.

From the market stalls and small shops in the city I purchased a lot of stuff for my eventual return to Blighty. There was a brightly coloured waistcoat decorated in an Aztec pattern, a crude silver and gold bracelet along with a pair of cufflinks made of the same metals and one extremely heavy onyx chessboard with its associated onyx chess pieces. Incidentally, the waistcoat still resides in my wardrobe to this day and the onyx chess set is in the living room but only one cufflink survives in a drawer somewhere or other in the house.

Strangely, these are all of the limited recollections I have of the events in Mexico City. I do not remember my trip back to Belize at all...similar to the memory loss I have about my return from Tikal...Why is it that you can always remember outgoing journeys to different places but never the return journey? This has happened to me on numerous occasions throughout my life!

Sadly, my Belizean adventure ended in February of 1974 and often a tune on the radio causes an avalanche of memories. Two records often played on the jukebox in the "Big C" were firstly, a record by The Beatles which I, surprisingly, had never heard until that particular time; the record "Come Together" completely blew my mind when it was first heard in that place. The second was the record "Me and Mrs Jones"...not normally my sort of sound but I always see a young

Pipil girl dancing with me on that dance floor while trying to sing the words of the record in faltering English into my ear. It always chokes me up. Other records that bring back memories of that time are: Mas Que Nada by Brazil 66, A Horse With No Name by America and Soul Makossa by Manu Dibango.

Before continuing my story I must finally clear up the chronology of some of the events that took place while I was in Belize. It kept bugging me about these event dates, so I decided to hunt for an old passport of mine that I knew was lying around somewhere. Finally, in an old metal box, at its bottom, and under some other old documents the elusive passport was discovered. Strange how the brain distorts memories of the distant past. To my absolute amazement, despite arriving in Belize on the 14th August in 1973, my passport tells me that I departed Belize exactly one week later via Melchor de Mencos on my trip to Tikal, and returned back into Belize through the same checkpoint two days later on the 23rd of August! It also tells me that I arrived in El Salvador on the 20th October and returned to Belize on the 23rd October and the trip to Mexico City that I was convinced had taken place in the early part of 1974 actually took place between the 28th November and 4th December 1973. Clearly dates are not my strong point but all the events whilst in Belize certainly did take place as described. In the metal box another relevant document was found, that of my Personal Medical Record. It detailed all of my inoculations whilst in the RAF...of no real importance here...but in the sleeve of this item I found two interesting business cards. One was from a Patricia Solis of the "Jaguar Inn" Tikal...she was the girl originally from Nottingham; and the other card was from a Ronald G. Ward, Vice Consul, British Embassy, San Salvador. A couple of scraps of paper also found at this time, included a receipt for a telegram I had sent to a Peter Pendleton, Salvador on the 30th October...he was, of course, the charge d'affaires in my story, and the other piece of paper was a receipt for a stay in the American Guesthouse, San Salvador; this included a little postage stamp for "un colon" as part of the legality of the document. Now that's cleared that up I will continue:

As stated earlier you never seem to remember your return journey from a place, and the trip home is no exception. The only things that do seem to come to mind are that the means of transport back to Blighty was a Hercules and my kit bag was very heavy...mainly due to a load of assorted souvenirs including that large onyx chess set bought in Mexico City.

We touched down at Brize Norton on a cold February evening and whether or not I stayed on camp overnight before going back, by bus and train, to see Mom and Dad in Birmingham, I'm not too sure. Anyway, when I arrived back home, amidst the usual homecoming greetings and present giving, Mom produced an article she had cut out of the Birmingham Evening Mail from a couple of months earlier. It showed a large picture of me in my K.D. uniform and around it a rather exaggerated and sensationalized story about my life in Belize after my large gambling windfall. I'd forgotten all about that journalist from the Birmingham Evening Mail who had come sniffing around the camp for a story on one of the more quieter afternoons there. Had I known he was going to write such inaccurate and sensationalized drivel I would not have talked to him at all. However, my parents seemed happy enough with it.

Chapter 7

After a brief period at home I was ready to face my next posting, and it proved to be the best posting I was ever to have in this country. It was a posting to the Central Flying School at RAF Little Rissington in the Cotswolds. The only problem for me with this camp was a lack of public transport to get me to and from this somewhat isolated aerodrome; so any trips back to my parents' home at weekends had to be done by the old hitch-hiking in uniform method or later on during my tour of duty there by a newly bought motorcycle.

Hitch-hiking in uniform has just reminded me about an anecdote I should have told you about earlier in this great rambling tale. It took place back in the late summer of 1969 shortly after I had left my basic training at RAF Swinderby and before my first posting to RAF Locking. Two of us from basic training decided to utilise the lull before our first respective proper postings to embark on a hitch-hiking trip across Denmark. We left from Harwich by ferry and crossed to Esbjerg on the west coast of Denmark. We probably chose Denmark to visit because of its reputation at that time as having a rather relaxed attitude to everything sexual and we probably hoped to get in on the "goings on" at some stage during our visit...unfortunately, we did not! What struck me about Denmark as we made our way, falteringly, across the country was that every house that we passed seemed to have a flagpole outside with an accompanying Danish flag on top. We once stopped at a commune in Odense where some kind "hippies" put us up for the night. We slept in our sleeping bags in a large room that was completely devoid of furniture and the only item in the whole room was a toilet pan in the corner that was occasionally visited by members of both sexes during the course of the night...weird or what! We travelled on to the capital, Copenhagen, thanks to the kindness of an assorted bunch of Danish motorists. We visited the Tivoli Gardens where we indulged in some of the attractions there, saw a mermaid by the sea, went to a place called Klampenberg where there were some other, long forgotten, attractions before starting back on our return journey. There is one other memory of the country that I have and that was that many of the newsagents there, at that time, had glass fronted dispensing machines outside their shops selling hard core porn magazines...we did not indulge, but what I, personally, found most distasteful was that these machines were at such a height from the ground that any child over the age of four or five could peer inside at the machine's disturbing contents...that was definitely out of order As previously stated earlier, the hypothesis of not remembering the details of a return journey continues here.

From the flashback to 1969 back to 1974 now and the stories surrounding my new posting at the wonderful RAF Little Rissington. As stated earlier this was the place where new pilots were trained and it was also the home of the world famous Red Arrows display team. This posting was in one of the most picturesque parts of the UK and the whole ethos around the camp was of a relaxed attitude towards the work we had to do. It seemed to me that there was an emphasis here on sport and healthy outdoor activities and there was a friendly rivalry between us in everything we did. I developed a bit of a friendship with another technician there; his name was Mick B., a slightly rotund fellow who, off duty, lived in married quarters with his wife and two children. He had a wonderfully relaxed west country manner and used to run around in his blue MG in the manner of an eligible young bachelor, much to his wife's obvious disapproval. We were continually competitive with each other whether it be with darts, dominoes or backgammon in the rest room or squash on the squash court. I continued my running whilst there and besides representing the station on the running track I also became involved in cross country events. We travelled to most RAF Stations in the south west to compete in cross country races and despite my fairly ordinary performances I did start to become more keen on this particular sport. On occasions Mick B. and I did go, in his blue MG, to horserace meetings, pubs and other assorted off-camp happenings much to the annoyance of his long-suffering wife. He liked his beer and I liked to think I had some sort of restraining effect on him in this area.

This was the time of enlightenment for me as I finally understood how a tunnel diode really worked...I think! Day-to-day work obviously involved the maintenance of the radar equipment at the camp and often immersed me in flow charts and other helpful guides when there was equipment failure. I was a FAULT-FINDER and a rectifier of problems in electrical circuitry and throughout the rest of my life this fault-finding habit has extended to all sorts of areas, though rectification of associated problems has not always been clear. Whilst at this station I got into Led Zeppelin and often played their stuff on a small cassette recorder I had, during off-duty periods, in my barrack block room. There were, of course, social interactions at the camp and at one of the dances my sergeant, a small, slightly pissed (at the time) Irishman, seeing me alone and somewhat down, pointed to his young attractive wife and suggested that she could certainly cheer me up...in hindsight, I now regret not taking him up on that offer! It was at this camp, I believe, I became a Corporal and my jump in rank could well have not stopped there, as the young Flight Lieutenant in charge of us asked me if I wanted to train to become an officer. After some thought I decided against the idea as I was too much of a hands-on person; I enjoyed what I did as a working technician.

It was at this station I decided to make a large logic board. It was about 30 inches by 24 inches and three inches deep. It was covered in a white coating and the symbols for the various different gates and generators underneath were painted on. Their little input and output sockets were available for interconnecting wires to be connected to in order to make a particular circuit function. It was completely original at that time and it was well received by my fellow technicians.

The RAF had given me assorted experiences, adventure and now it was to encourage me into a proper education with the Open University, a gift I am eternally grateful for! I believe they paid for the courses and gave me time off to attend the relevant summer schools at the different universities.

One of my enduring memories of being at this station was a flight with a Flight Lieutenant Schofield "doing circuits-and-bumps" over the airfield. Flight Lieutenant Schofield was a flying instructor who had a sick motorcycle. He knew I knew something about those machines, so if I repaired his motorcycle he would give me a flight in his two-seater Jet Provost. I had to go through all the pre-flight stuff, like how to use your ejector seat in the event of an emergency, and after being given these instructions, one evening, we got going. I was surprised that I was allowed to land the dual control aircraft during one of the circuits of the airfield but it was, of course, done so under strict supervision. At the end of the flight we taxied to dispersal and I was told to pull a certain lever under my seat to release myself. Unfortunately I released the emergency oxygen supply instead and rendered that plane unusable for the rest of that evening...Help!

Regrettably, in 1976 the MOD decided, in its wisdom, to close down RAF Little Rissington ...why I will never know... anyway some of us were charged with the task of dismantling all the electronic gear for transportation to other sites and as we removed equipment from the conning tower that last summer we replaced the items with grow bags and after a short period the place was like a jungle, full of tomato, pepper, and courgette plants. Our last defiant gesture for closing down this wonderful station!

Chapter 8

My Open University education continued at my next RAF Station and this posting turned out to be the final one in my RAF career. The station I was required to go to was RAF Binbrook in the Lincoln Wolds. It was a station that was as far away from the joys of Little Rissington as you could get. I was to spend the next five years on a camp that I was never completely at home in.

RAF Binbrook was a station in the Lincoln Wolds where Lightnings flew from. It was always cold in the winter and not much warmer in the summer (or is that just my prejudice talking?). Fortunately, one way or the other I spent a fair amount of time away from the camp; there were trips to various universities for summer schools, a trip to a course on a new radar system, frequent outings to athletics meetings and eventually periodic trips to live off-camp in my own house. The first course that I had taken with the OU was a foundation one in technology for which I received a full credit distinction. That course had taken place mostly while I was at Little Rissington with the summer school being at Warwick University. The next two courses I took simultaneously; one was a full credit science foundation course in science and the other was a half credit in maths. This arrangement required my attendance at two summer schools during the summer of 1977 and the RAF kindly allowed me the time off for both. There was a summer school at Bath University for my maths and a summer school at Reading University for the science. Now this is where my life gets a bit complicated again. You see at Reading University I met a fellow student; her name was Di L. We were attracted to each other and started a rather long distance relationship, in which odd weekends were spent together at different venues and sometimes, intermittently, at a hotel. It was easy enough for me as I was a single man again (from way back), but Di L. had a young son J.L. and was still in a married but loosening relationship with J.L.'s father. Despite these personal distractions I still managed a full credit distinction in science and a grade 2 pass in mathematics.

In 1978 my time in the RAF was about to end as my nine years contract was up, but a promise of a golden handshake at the end of an additional three years along with a pension once I had reached the age of 60, decided me to extend until 1981. I started a course with the OU in 1978 in geology/geochemistry and during a summer school at Durham University I inexplicably decided to kick the OU into touch. I can only assume that I needed a break to explore a more permanent relationship with a newly divorced Di L. We looked around for cheap properties in the Binbrook area but nothing was within our price range and the thought of living in nearby Grimsby, 12 miles away, turned my stomach. I'm not sure how, but a cheap property in a village just north of Gainsborough, over 27 miles away from Binbrook, became of interest to us, a place, maybe, where we could live the "Good Life". It was an end of terrace cottage in a state of severe disrepair, hence its price of £3000. Clearly, transport to and from my place of work at Binbrook was going to be a serious problem for me but I believe the idea was for Di L. and her son to take residence in the rundown building to start with, while I remained in my quarters at Binbrook during the week and visited at free weekends to work on the property to help make it more habitable.

Life at Binbrook whilst on duty there proceeded as normal and I still kept up with my running by representing my station at various athletics meetings and also entered a few road races around this time. I recall one particular 10 mile road race, between two RAF Stations in the London area, which I completed in, a somewhat pedestrian, 62 minutes. Around this time there was also an excursion to the Isle of Wight in order to be taught the ins and outs of a new piece of radar equipment, ACR 430. It was a course at the Plessey Co. situated at Cowes and the journey there encompassed my first ever trip on a hovercraft. I can't remember anything about my stay in Cowes except for a vague recollection of visiting a picture house somewhere with a fellow trainee and a girl he had picked up from our hotel, where she worked as a receptionist.

At some stage I managed to get a loan from my bank to fund the purchase of the property in that village just north of Gainsborough, and it was not long before Di L. and J.L. moved in. In order to remedy my transport problems to and from Binbrook, whilst in Birmingham one weekend, I purchased this second-hand monstrous Russian motorbike and sidecar. Anyone who has ever ridden a motorbike and sidecar for the first time will understand the problems I had driving it across Birmingham in heavy evening traffic. This monster was an absolute nightmare to steer and on two occasions I actually mounted the curb, once stopping inches from the trunk of a large tree. The amount of abuse I received from fellow motorists on that journey back to the village was unbelievable...but I got there...eventually! Luckily practice does make perfect and over the next few weeks the monster was tamed.

The end of terrace cottage was extremely basic; there was a living room and a small kitchen downstairs and one large bedroom and one small bedroom upstairs. Alongside the main body of this old building, but slightly set back, a more recently built building containing a bathroom and separate toilet, had been added. These ablutions were accessed via the adjacent living room. The original cottage had a door at the side, in front of where the toilet and bathroom now stood, but this mostly glass door had been permanently closed to form a large "window" and access to the cottage was now by a front door. Entering this front door, the stairs to the upper rooms were directly in front of you, the doorless entrance to the small kitchen was on your left and the entrance to the living room was on your right. At the top of the stairs was a very small "landing" area of about six square feet; the small bedroom was on your left directly above the small kitchen and on your right was the main bedroom directly above the living room below. It was certainly an uncomplicated structure and was to become my home for the next nine years or so. The surrounds of the house were not quite that simple, however. Looking towards the front of the house you would see to the left that the building was attached to one large pebble-dashed cottage that had clearly been three smaller dwellings in the past. This larger cottage had a garden that stretched totally in front of our place, and our garden was offset to one side next to a large farmer's field. All along the back of this row of originally four dwellings was someone else's back garden...complicated or what! Off to the right of our cottage, as you looked at it, and beyond our added on bathroom, but next to it, there was an old coal shed; joined to that there was a large greenhouse with vine and beyond that, and joined to it, was a sizeable garage made of breeze blocks with a transparent plastic roof. Finally, the way of getting to our cottage from the road was through the garden of the pebble-dashed cottage next door or by the (more often used) dirt track that led from the road to the doors of our breeze block garage.

During my last year at Binbrook I had started to reside on a more or less permanent basis at the cottage. It was hard some winter mornings getting up at 5am in total darkness, then trying to get the monster to start, and having eventually done so, travelling on untreated snow-covered roads the 27 miles to Binbrook. The machine was difficult to get up those hills at the best of times, but in winter I was often lurching all over the road to try and get some grip from somewhere; and on many mornings when I finally did arrive on site I was the subject of much laughter from my mates as my moustache usually had icicles hanging from it!

Around this time my mother – and, incredibly, my father – were witnesses in a Birmingham Registry Office to my marriage to Di L. He obviously now thought that by my mid-thirties I knew what I was doing, and on the couple of occasions he had met Di she had made quite a favourable impression on him.

Now, throughout my life my family have always had dogs...there was Chipper, a brown terrier, in the fifties and sixties; Smartie, a black smooth haired mongrel, in the sixties and seventies; and so when Di suggested we have a dog to keep her and her son company while I was working at Binbrook, I was in total agreement with her.

We set off in the monster to a dog pound just north of Lincoln, and looking around the caged animals it was like being in a sweet shop for me, as I would have taken all of them home, but the dog that appealed to us most was a mostly white mongrel (with a few brown and black patches) called Sam. We passed in front of his cage and we both saw a really friendly dog so happy to see us, and as we walked away to organise his release we turned and saw him totally collapse with disappointment...it was a real tear-jerker. The open-topped sidecar of my motorbike had to house Di and an excited young dog on our bumpy journey back to the cottage and Sam spent the first hour or so of his arrival there, sniffing around and generally getting acquainted with his new surroundings. Of course, he had plenty to sniff at, as by then, I think, we had half a dozen chickens in an "ark" in the garden, a hutch full of rabbits, and an old apple tree and an old pear tree that he could use to relieve himself on after his long trip from Lincoln. The number of rabbits we had was unintentional...there was originally one black rabbit bought as a pet for Di's young man, J. L, but it appears that at some stage a wild rabbit had entered the hutch, or more likely its pen outside, by some means or other, and mated with our, now discovered, FEMALE black rabbit. The product of this union were four surviving offspring of different colours, namely ginger, white, black, and black and white; and were named by us as: Any, Tom, Dick and Harry.

The re-occurring problem with RAF Binbrook was that there always seemed to be an exercise going on. This essentially meant that the station was in "lockdown" and getting off the camp was almost impossible for the whole duration of the exercise, which could be for several days at a time. Guards were posted at strategic points around the camp particularly at the main gate and any movement by personnel through the entrance was severely scrutinized. Now, wouldn't you know it, one day before my final day in the air force was due, they started a snap exercise and I was on site at the time. Clearly on May 27th 1981, as far as I was concerned, I became a civilian again and nothing was going to stop me and my belongings going through that main gate and back to my cottage home. Rightly or wrongly I walked straight through the main gate, ignoring the guard with his rifle shouting "stop or I'll shoot" and continued on my way in the hope that he didn't have a bullet in the wretched thing. That was the end of my formal time in the air force but, of course, I was still a reservist for the next three years as an undertaking of my last re-engagement had specified.

Finally, I don't wish to sound like a cheerleader for the RAF but, in hindsight, the service gave me a trade, different experiences, adventure and the opportunity for further education...having said all that I was extremely lucky, in my particular twelve years, not to have been involved in any serious conflict. As far as a trade is concerned in civvy street, my "exemplary" character on discharge, my "outstanding ability" on my fitters course and a glowing report from my commanding officer clearly led to the approach by letter from the Royal Signals and Radar Establishment in Malvern. Now this is one of those key moments in one's life (again) when there were two ways to go...I think I probably made the wrong decision this time in that I rejected any idea of moving to picturesque Malvern in favour of staying in my cosy little cottage in Lincolnshire.

Chapter 9

The cottage over the years had now become more habitable. Di's elderly father helped me re-roof the property and I lined all the walls. I re-established the old side entrance and built a long thin conservatory on its outside (and in front of the bathroom) that extended to the greenhouse. We had now christened the place Vine Cottage in honour of the Black Hamburg that grew in the greenhouse and which provided us with abundant fruit every year. The sizeable garden was essentially oblong in shape but a corner of it contained a dilapidated old barn which was the property of the farmer who lived on the other side of our nearby field. With some of the money I received from the RAF when I left, I bought the ruin of a barn from the farmer opposite for £350. I pulled it down and expanded the growing area of my garden. We grew a lot of different stuff and there was a large area of blackcurrant bushes planted so that we could make loads of long lasting jam. Interestingly, there was a well at the top of the garden and whilst trying to make it deeper one hot summer I discovered a huge number of belemnite calcitic guards. I assume that when this area had been under water at some stage, they had been selectively deposited at this site for some reason.

The winter after we got Sam, whilst leaving the only shop in the village, a Co-Op, we found him a companion. It was outside on a snow-covered pavement that we spotted a shivering little brown and white whippet trying to get into the shop for warmth. There was no collar and he had clearly been abandoned. We couldn't refuse him and we took him home to join Sam...we called him Gravity for some reason that now escapes me. Sam was your sure and steady fellow, Gravity was fast, impulsive and mad. He lived his life in the fast lane and would often run into the house at speed and throw himself onto a sleeping Sam with complete abandon. It would be true to say that Sam tolerated Gravity rather than ever befriending him. Gravity had to be put down after only a few years of high speed living because of the rapid spread of lymphosarcoma that severely restricted his movement...it kills me to think of it!

The winters were cold and I don't think we had an open fire so we must have relied on a few small wall gas heaters dotted around the building to keep us warm. There was one in the bathroom, one in the living room, one in the kitchen and one on the small landing at the top of the stairs that served both bedrooms. They didn't give out that much heat so we tended to keep plenty of cloths on. We usually celebrated Christmas quietly; there was a tree and the usual decorative trimmings and I can't remember a television...but I suppose there must have been one. I do remember being introduced to Carmina Burana by Di at some time and it always reminds me when I hear part of it played before the start of some football matches, of cold but cosy Christmases in Vine Cottage.

Having been politically neutral throughout my life I started to become very aware of stuff that was going on around me. I was on the dole, Di received no income and despite the frugal life we were leading there were outgoings that had to be addressed. School uniforms had to be paid for, gas bills and electricity bills had to be settled and we weren't completely self-sustaining food-wise. So I became increasingly desperate for work; I was rejected as a postman for being "over-qualified" and after still not finding work locally after successfully completing a long course in Technical Authorship in the late summer of 1982 at Eaton Hall in Nottinghamshire, my anti-establishment views were becoming more pronounced. This was at a time when I was beginning to get the feeling that Di was starting to fall out of love with the "Good Life" and when the Thatcher administration was getting into full swing with its "Londoncentric" doctrines that rewarded the already well-off at the expense of the majority...particularly the Northern majority. Things came to a head on the 2nd anniversary of my discharge from the RAF when in a fit of angst I put a house brick through the local job centre window; a job centre that had been totally unhelpful to me. After doing the deed I immediately presented myself at the local police station and confessed to my illegal act. The "old school" station sergeant was not pleased and I was subsequently charged with the offence. The station sergeant was not the only one that was not pleased, Di was livid...our hard earned standing in this tight-knit community was now in tatters! This did not matter one jot to me and I was certainly never going to pay the fine imposed on me by the local court! Di said that if I went to jail she would leave me...I was sentenced to 14 days imprisonment in Lincoln jail for non-payment of a fine.

Lincoln jail was a disgusting place, there were three people to a small cell and you could not sleep at night with the noisy shouts and yells of some of the more "unstable" prisoners. By my estimation I think a good third of the internees should have been in mental institutions rather than prison. Luckily I became a "trustee" which allowed me out of my cell to wander around below the rest of the prison cells picking up "shit parcels" thrown out of their cells by incontinent or disaffected prisoners...what a privilege! After a couple of days my one telephone call to Di was spent expressing my total disgust for the place and how I was finding it very difficult to come to terms with my incarceration. Money was raised via Di's parents, the fine was paid and I was released from prison. However, it was not long before Di and her son left me and then I was left in Vine Cottage alone, with just my faithful Sam and nutty Gravity.

For the next couple of years I was left to muse on the meaning of life, the universe and everything; I lost Gravity during this period.

Whilst taking the dogs on their daily walk along the raised bank that stretched out for miles alongside the river Trent, I had to pass the noisy garden of a semi-detached Edwardian property. The noise emanated from four large white geese, a dopey Afghan and an Irish Wolfhound. I often stopped at the gate of this house so that all the dogs could say "hello" to each other and it was not long before I became friends with the owner, an elderly lady called Doreen. We soon found we shared common interests in self-sufficiency, current affairs and Scrabble and it eventually became part of my routine to visit her with Sam in the afternoons for tea, biscuits and games of Scrabble.

It was during one of these afternoon visits in September of 1985 that the very first seed may have been planted in my mind concerning the way that things were. There was a newspaper on a table whose headlines broadcasted the news that there had been an earthquake in Mexico City killing large numbers of people in its wake. It was a story that, had I not isolated myself completely from "Thatcherworld" over the previous few days, I may have picked up on sooner, but it was a story that would torment my thought processes for some time to come. The fact that earthquakes were occurring all the time in one part of the world or another should not have made these headlines particularly significant...but I had been in this particular place, I had walked those very streets; streets that were now in total ruin! I explained to Doreen that I had visited the place while I was stationed in Belize and over the next hour or so while playing Scrabble recounted my exploits to her while I was there...at least those exploits that were seemly to recount to a woman of her, seemingly, parochial perspective! After that September afternoon visit to Doreen's, Sam and I returned to our isolated retreat. I have visions of it being a mild still evening with tractors working nearby fields, swallows swooping overhead and the smells of late summer filling my nostrils, and as I lay in bed that night listening to the mice scurrying about behind the false walls of my abode, I mulled over the thought of how a recent earthquake in Mexico City could be linked in some way to my presence there 12 years earlier. Was it that the "Grim Reaper" was chasing me throughout the whole of my life, eventually catching up with me and overtaking me on the day of my demise? I, probably, fell asleep exploring these ideas with, as usual, Sam snoring quietly in the background at the foot of my bed.

Life continued to proceed at its slow leisurely pace throughout the coming months; work was still non-existent in "Thatcherworld", parents back in Brum were not staving off the ravages of time too well and I still remained an "outsider" in a village I had lived in for seven years. That autumn was not too dissimilar to previous years; garden vegetables and fruits needed to be harvested and stored, egg production continued to tail off as the nights drew in and more mice than ever were coming in off the fields to invade the cottage. I spent most nights getting up at all hours to release humanely trapped mice at the bottom of the garden knowing full well that they would, in all probability, be back in the cottage before I was! Still it gave Sam a chance to have a sniff around and relieve himself, and kept me in touch with rural Lincolnshire nightlife.

It was the loss of over 250 soldiers in an air accident in December of 1985 that re-kindled my interest in possible links between the present and the past. The plane crash that took all of those lives took place in Gander, Canada ... once again a place that I had passed through on my way to Belize over 12 years earlier.

Now, many "God-botherers" seem to have some sort of epiphany at some stage in their lives; well I had an epiphany at this time without involving a god of any sort. It was a sudden revelation indeed, which I shall now try to explain as best as I can.

I postulated that there was some sort of boundary or line between existence in this world and non-existence (conveniently a straight line) and at birth we emerge from the world of non-existence below into the world of existence above. We then "rise" to a point halfway through our lives when we are furthest away from non-existence before descending, inextricably, back to that boundary line at our death. Now since I have always dealt with sine waves in my working life it is nice to theorize that the pathway of our life can be represented by a similar waveform; and whether it continues to look like a sine wave during non-existence before re-emerging once again as part of the same sine wave at a later time somewhere along the boundary, I will let the reader decide! Anyway, you may wonder what all this stuff has got to do with the events around my Belizean adventure in 1973 and those events that took place in 1985 (sort of deadly echoes of the past stuff)...well this is where it gets a bit tricky... Now, considering our absolute position in space and time are continually changing, it does take a leap of "faith" to accept any sort of linkage between the past and the (then) present, but the two positions on my lifeline surrounding my trip to Belize are compatible with the reverse position of events in 1985. Yes in 1973 it was Gander followed by Mexico City whereas in 1985 it is Mexico City followed by Gander...meaning I have passed my mid-point and in 1985 I'm on my way down back towards non-existence. There are clearly incidents of disaster and death continually occurring throughout the world all the time, so the belief is that these events relate to the pasts of other people's lives. The corollary from all of this stuff is that I, probably, ain't going to make eighty...but who knows.

It was, of course, about this time that I scrawled my message to the world on my garage wall about us being a product of our genetics and past and present environment only, mostly in angst against all the "mumbo jumbo" merchants of all organised religious groups that were totally responsible for most of the conflicts in the world. They alone were responsible for setting peoples against peoples...oh sorry... along with politicians, of course!

Chapter 10

Anyway back to the story; 1986 came along with a visit from my brother Dennis in the spring of that year to say that Mom was now suffering from bowel cancer and with Dad's Parkinson's getting worse maybe I should sell my cottage and move back down to Birmingham to look after both of them. All of my siblings agreed that this was the best course of action as they all had their own family commitments and I was the only one that was now unattached. This time in my life is really confusing, though, as a photograph I have of a heavily bearded me with my frail mom taken at the cottage by Dennis, I think, shows Sam and Gravity in the picture and on the back of the photo the date 1986 had been written. However, further analysis concludes that the date on the back is incorrect and that the photograph is from a previous visit by Dennis with Mom a couple of years earlier...the date written is in my present partner's hand and I had probably given her false information about the picture. After consideration of my family's plea I did decide to put the house up for sale and then tried to dissuade a young couple from buying it with tales of mouse infestation...it did not succeed and the property was sold to them for £14,500. During a return visit to the property from Birmingham to tie up some loose ends I was told the shocking news that my friend Doreen had suddenly died and her funeral was to be in a few days' time. When I got back to Birmingham I, rather extravagantly, hired a Rolls Royce to take me to and from the church where the service was to be held; in some strange way I felt she deserved the gesture.

Life back in Brum was desperate; Mom, despite radiotherapy, was getting worse, Dad, who was always full of angst, was becoming more anti everything and the Macmillan lady was inclined to a more religious view of proceedings. On one dreadful Saturday evening whilst downstairs with Dad the last gasp of my mother's 81 years of life was heard...it was unbearable!

The day of the funeral the heavens opened in sympathy; the rain was torrential and I spent the whole of the proceedings in tears...probably the saddest day of my life.

The days and weeks that followed were equally as awful; Dad simply could not cope with the loss of his partner after over 60 years of marriage; I tried to cope with his daily needs but his initial sad demeanour turned into his usual anger and I became his "whipping boy". He complained to a visiting social worker that I had been manhandling him, which, of course, was totally untrue, but naturally there had to be a "stewards enquiry", and after all of the associated nonsense my sympathetic siblings along with the social workers decided it would be best if he were to be placed in an old people's home. About this time I contracted measles, I recall, which I put down to the stress of recent events; however it is fair to say that other health problems were starting to manifest themselves. Like my siblings I was to be increasingly plagued with our genetic auto-immune problems. John, the youngest of my twin brothers, had suffered from diabetes (and had to inject insulin) brought on from the stress of worrying about his wife's toxaemia in late pregnancy. Dennis, the other twin, suffered from ankylosing spondylitis and Joan, my sister, suffered from bouts of diverticulitis. I had suffered from iritis on occasions in the past and, like Dennis, was later in my life, to be diagnosed with ankylosing spondylitis and, on a couple of instances, diverticulitis like my sister.

Attempts at purchasing my family home from Birmingham Council failed and so I decided to have a narrowboat built in order to live a rural existence on a canal somewhere with my faithful old friend Sam, who accompanied me throughout all my recent tribulations.

The boat was built in Doncaster and on its completion Dennis drove me and Sam up to collect it. Sam and I now set out on a new adventure in driving the boat down to the Midlands, where I could be closer to my nearby relatives.

The boat was just a metal shell with an old reconditioned Lister engine. It had no ballast and it was my intention to fit the boat out when I settled in my final destination, which I had decided was going to be somewhere near Tamworth.

Anyone who has had the misfortune to try and steer a ballast-less boat in strong winds will understand the problems I had on my faltering journey down towards Tamworth. We left Thorne in Doncaster and travelled along the Thorne to Keadby canal. This is a very wide navigation canal, very exposed and at this time a passageway for quite large vessels. It often took all of my strength to keep my ballast-less vessel away from the bank of the canal and the sides of passing large vessels, as the wind was very strong at that time. At Keadby we gained access onto the river Trent and our trip upstream included passing by the very village Sam and I had lived in a couple of years earlier. I felt he was sniffing the air a bit more than normal as we passed by, but that may have been my imaginings. We continued our journey through Newark and towards Holme Pierrepont, where the river runs alongside the world famous rowing centre. At night-times on our journey I had a mattress that fitted on the boat's base plate (and between its raised cross beams) to sleep on, and Sam had his own little wooden sleeping box. Food was acquired at various mooring-up points along our route and there was an emergency bucket for use as a toilet when necessary. We passed through Nottingham (close to Trent Bridge Cricket Ground) and somewhere around Long Eaton we got onto the Trent Mersey Canal. Now for some time along our travels the old Lister engine had been overheating quite badly, so I had to contact the boatbuilder to get some sort of remedial action done. I was forced to moor-up at Shardlow Marina, at great expense, to await someone coming down from Doncaster to fix the problem. It was over two weeks before anyone actually arrived at the marina to do the required work. The guys that turned up decided to cut two blooming great holes in both sides of the engine compartment in order to keep a good flow of air over the engine. They welded on several cross pieces to each aperture in a louvred configuration to keep the elements out, and I, eventually, continued on my way. The modifications proved to be only a slight improvement, but since I was going to be using the boat as more of a domicile than a cruising vessel, I decided not to make a big issue of things. We went through stinky Burton-on-Trent and on to Fradley Junction, where a quick turn left along the Birmingham and Fazeley canal followed by another left turn along the Coventry Canal took us to our final mooring up point at Alvecote marina, just east of Tamworth.

Peter Pratt was the owner of the small marina; he was a short, fairly rotund chap with plenty of blond facial hair and a serious long term plan. His plan was to buy the large flat area of land on the opposite side of the canal and build a huge marina there. (His dream would, eventually, become reality, but Peter, tragically, would die long before he could see the large residential boatyard in full operation.) He owned a few narrowboats which he hired out on a weekly basis as one source of income and relied as well on mooring fees from one or two of his more permanent residents of which I was, now, to become one. He did also run a small souvenir shop and had a workshop to help with any repairs that any of his residents or any passers-by may need to be done to their boat. His wife also assisted him with the running of the place and they did have a young male part-time helper who did most of the dirty work and whose name now completely escapes me. Fortunately my brother Dennis passed on to me my father's carpentry tools to help my fitting out of my boat and Peter Pratt supplied all the required stuff (at a price) that was needed to make my 40 foot narrowboat habitable. Ballast was fitted onto the bottom base plate and then covered over with sheets of marine plywood. The bottom halves of the sides of the boat were covered in the same marine ply and the top halves of the boat's sides were covered with lengths of tongue and groove pine in the traditional manner. A bed was built at the front end and a TV table with associated shelves fabricated around the foot of the bed for easy viewing whilst lying down in the bed. At the front end, as well, a wood burner was incorporated and built onto a raised, tile-covered dais. Windows were fitted throughout the whole of the narrowboat, of course, and front and rear doors fitted. The central part of the boat housed a toilet and hidden holding tank capable of being pumped out, a shower unit with a hand pump to clear the associated tray and a small hand basin that discharged into the holding tank, I think. There was also a large mirror that had once graced my parents' bedroom back in Birmingham. All these central features stood to one side of a narrow corridor that connected the front of the boat to the rear "kitchen" area; this area contained a gas fired fridge, a small gas cooker, a sink and a small food preparation area. The boat had a built-in gas bottle holder and water tank at the front and a large battery and diesel tank in the engine compartment at the rear; both these areas were outside the living section and all the necessary pipework and cabling was hidden behind the side panels. After being fitted out the craft was named Floss after my late mother. Sam had his sleeping area under the TV table but often jumped up onto the bottom of my bed on cold nights.

To help fund the cost of all this stuff I found a job at a plastics factory in Tamworth as a maintenance fitter, which was an easy moped ride away to get to. This particular job only lasted about a year or so before I moved onto a better position at a newly opened Sainsbury supermarket. I was now described as a maintenance engineer and my work covered repairs to almost everything mechanical or electrical throughout the store. My employer was not Sainsburys itself but a maintenance company based in Coventry contracted to the supermarket.

In 1991 my brother Dennis informed me that my father had died in the old people's home he had been placed in four years earlier. I believe my siblings, particularly my sister, had visited him on a fairly regular basis, but, shamefully, I had visited him just twice in all the time that he was in the home. I remember absolutely nothing about his funeral.

At this time and throughout the rest of my life my philosophy was to take as little from the planet as I deemed reasonable. I, definitely, did **not fly**, despite 12 years in the air force, I did **not eat red meat** and, apart from the occasional use of a small moped, only ever **used public transport** to get me around. I was (and still remain) **NOT** a member of the consumer society. All these beliefs were because I saw what was coming a long way off, unlike the politicians of the day.

Anyway back to the story; life on the narrowboat was now comfortable and Sam had the canal towpath to wander along at will, and it was on one of these wanderings during the school summer holidays that we came across a pair of young girls. They made a fuss of Sam and I got into a conversation with them. I think the blonde one had found a key and she wondered what to do with it. I suggested that she should hand it at Peter Pratt's shop for collection by the unfortunate owner, as this was the only place for miles where the key could be handed in. We continued to chat and the girls said they had nothing to do during the holidays primarily because of a lack of cash. Now my income at this time was reasonable and my outgoings minimal so in a fit of generosity I suggested that on Saturday mornings they could come and clean my boat for a small remuneration, provided that their parents agreed. The following Saturday morning they duly arrived and I set them to work. The brunette was called Kelly and the blonde Suzi and they soon became regular visitors to the boat on Saturday mornings. I think at some stage Suzi's mom, Pam (and her younger sister, Julie) came to make sure everything was kosher for her pre-teenage daughter. At this time the boat had another regular visitor in the form of a tortoise-shell coloured, feral cat, that I christened Tiger. Sam and Tiger got on OK and they both often shared the bed with me on cold nights. One of my enduring memories of this time took place in the early hours of the morning on one hot summer's night when I was lying in my bed trying to sleep and was forced to listen to the sounds of a rave taking place in a field more than a mile away. The sound most remembered was of Black Box's Ride On Time which must have been played at least four or five times during that night... if not more!

Having enjoyed my work at Sainsburys things were soon to change as my employer wanted me to learn to drive so that I could be moved from shop to shop within the Midlands area. Since my original contract talked about being a permanent engineer at the Tamworth store, I was loath to take a driving test to become mobile, particularly as I hated cars and what they were doing to the environment. I also doubted the wisdom of my employer's strategy so I dug my heels in for as long as I could, but to my eternal shame I capitulated and took lessons. This eventually resulted in a failed driving test for "not progressing"... that is not driving fast enough! (I suppose I must, subconsciously, have been remembering just tootling along in the Land Rover whilst driving around the airfield all those years ago). I took my employer to tribunal and ignoring an offer of a financial settlement at "half-time", I made the **big** mistake in the second half of blowing my own trumpet on the work that I was doing at Sainsburys...nobody but nobody likes a smart-ass, not even the supposedly "impartial" adjudicators.....I lost the appeal and my job.

Around this time Sam, whose health had been declining for some time, had become completely immobile and I had to take the wretched decision of calling in the vet. I stood outside the boat as the vet did what was required and once again I was in a state of complete distress... my wailing could be heard throughout the boatyard and as is the case with my father dealing with my mother's death, sadness turned to anger and bitterness...no one could approach me for days afterwards. Now whenever anyone in our family gets stressed it usually leads to health problems...it's clearly a genetic thing; as a result of Sam's death I became severely depressed and, unusually for me, started to suffer from painful headaches. Despite the occasional visits of Tiger, the cat, I was completely alone, as I was the only one left moored up in the boatyard at that time. One dark evening I was so totally down that I sought comfort at the council house where Pam and her two young girls lived, a place that I had visited on and off on several previous occasions. Pam took me in on a more permanent basis that evening and I struck up a relationship with Pam that has lasted for well over twenty seven years now!

Pam's circumstances were similar to mine in that we had both been married twice and were now both unattached. She was a scouser born and bred, but without the accent, and had led quite a chequered and varied life mostly whilst attached to the Foreign Office. Her early secretarial life in Liverpool had given way to becoming the wife of a member of the Foreign Office and she subsequently found herself accompanying her first husband to both Kenya and Iran. In Kenya she gave birth to a son, Steven, and then a daughter, Helen, and later all four of them lived for some time in Iran together. At some stage for reasons that have always remained unexplained, and of which I have never had any wish to understand, she found herself back in the UK with another member of the Foreign Office, without her children. She eventually married the guy and gave birth to the two children now living with her, namely, Suzi and Julie. Her second husband became an alcoholic with rather nasty tendencies who was living away from Pam when I arrived on the scene. At that time Pam was making ends meet as a part-time child minder and at some point later she started to work at a local school as a teaching assistant. Despite my disastrous co-habiting with three females on a previous occasion, this time we all managed to get on with each other reasonably well. After leaving Sainsburys I needed to find other work and eventually found a job as a maintenance engineer at the Belfry Hotel some six miles away. I had two means of getting there, one was by bike along the towpath of the Birmingham and Fazeley canal and the other along the Coleshill road by moped.

Now that I was living with Pam on a permanent basis in a house whose location I was not completely happy with, I decided to sell my boat to raise enough money for a deposit on another house, and one day I had a dealer come down from the north with £7,500 in cash in his hand and the boat was sold... at quite a loss!

Chapter 11

My work at the Belfry was varied, from involving myself in the minutiae of the building management systems to clearing blocked toilets, but my regular early morning duty was replacing any bulbs or lamps that were no longer working. My daily journey around the corridors and rooms of this very large hotel on my "bulb run" resulted in me passing by, or occasionally chatting to, a number of the country's most famous celebrities. They came from the world of showbusiness, acting, athletics, football but primarily from the world of golf. The hotel was and still is a golfing hotel; it has hosted the Ryder Cup on four occasions and countless pro/am tournaments involving many different celebrities. I will not name-drop here but my maintenance "room service" has led me to chat to (or be chastised by) some of the most famous people in the land.

Whilst working at the Belfry, Pam and I managed to find a semi-detached house within our budget; it required only a relatively small deposit, which, of course, came from the sale of my boat. It is the house that we live in today but when we first arrived it was in a disgusting state. The previous deceased male owner had been a heavy smoker and all of the rooms were coated in nicotine and the property had not been properly maintained. A lot of work was needed to make it habitable and a fellow maintenance guy from the Belfry with good plumbing skills helped us enormously, and my electrical knowhow also came into play. With the aid of another Belfry co-worker (an expongo) our belongings were transferred from the council house we had been living in to our new private dwelling. Despite the fact that we had only moved a couple of miles both the girls were fairly "anti" the move because they were going to lose all their old friends but we all coped ...eventually. During those early years in the new house I built a large conservatory at the back which remains to this day. Its brickwork is as good as new and its wooden skeleton is still intact apart from some slight erosion in one corner...I must do something about that! All the double-glazed windows are OK and the plastic roof remains fairly undisturbed, probably because its northern aspect and shelter from the sun's glare by the house itself has prevented its decay. Towards the end of the nineties we purchased a computer and this was later to become instrumental in one "strange" reunion...this one involving Pam; I, too, would encounter yet another "strange" reunion but that is for later in this tale.

In 1997 I voted for the first time in my life at the age of fifty-two; with my strong anti-Tory views that had been well-established in the early eighties, I was persuaded to vote for Tony Blair. It only took a couple of years before I realized I had been conned by a "used-car salesman"... for that is all he was and continues to be. His tinkering with Clause 4 destroyed the Labour party that my father knew and helped to create the fragmented party that we see today, a party full of hypocrites and bigots...but in the end they are all politicians...they are all people professing they stand up for, and represent, groups of other peoples but in the final analysis are only concerned (understandably?) with their own individual well-being! As you can see I have started to become more politicised by this time.

Around the millennium period there were a whole batch of funerals that had to be attended. In 1997, I think, my sister-in-law, Pat, died of cancer, followed a year later by John, her husband, who, essentially, died of a broken heart (he just let himself go and was no longer taking his insulin); and in 2001 Pam's father, Fred, died, leaving us enough money to pay off our outstanding mortgage; also in the early part of this century my sister's husband, Bernard, died (a funeral that I did not attend because I was suffering from a severe bout of labyrinthitis) and in 2004 Pam's aunty Sheila died...five funerals in under seven years ...all very personal tragedies...but in 2001, of course, a more public tragedy was to occur.

At the Belfry in 2001 we were beginning to prepare for that year's Ryder Cup; I spent part of my time laying in electrical cable to new temporary out-buildings that were needed for the administrative work required during the competition, and there was a general excitement and anticipation around the whole place. I was actually re-tuning a television in one of the rooms when images of planes flying into skyscrapers filled the screen. At first I thought I had tuned into a disaster movie, but it was not too long before I established these were **real** events taking place. Shortly after the initial shock of seeing all of this insanity taking place, the hotel was full of people frantically running around trying to speculate about what it all meant for the forthcoming Ryder Cup. It was not long before we knew it was to be postponed and all our preparatory work had been in vain. I left the hotel before the re-scheduled Ryder Cup took place there the following year. The reasons for my departure from the hotel were primarily concerned with the appointment of a familiar "outside" engineer to be my boss. This guy had periodically been called in, usually when I was not on duty, to clear glitches in the building management system and more often than not, after he had been brought in, it was me who ending up clearing the fault!...It really pissed me off...and the thought of him now being my boss was too much!

Now back to Pam's "strange" reunion. On our computer, one of those old heavy monsters, Pam had been told to try Friends Re-united to get in touch with long lost friends. She put in her maiden name and said she had spent some time in Nairobi and she was contacted, out of the blue, one day by her daughter Helen's partner who, at some stage, had even hired a private detective to try and find Pam. Helen and her brother Steven soon got in touch with Pam and here is the "strangest" thing in that, despite travelling all over the world with their father, both Helen and Steven had settled in, of all places, **Birmingham** (a place where we soon met up for the very first time)...spooky or what! This all took place in 2002 when both Pam's children were unmarried, but since then they have both married their partners and both have two children each; Helen has a boy and a girl, Steven has two boys.

The "revenge" attack on Iraq by the Americans showed us all that we needed to know about the "used-car salesman" Blair. Here you had a Labour party leader getting into bed with a republican president... unbelievable!... And all the subsequent nonsense about weapons of mass destruction only cemented my views of the man and his so-called New Labour. I am told he needs praise for arranging the Good Friday Agreement; well my understanding is that it was the late Mo Mowlam who did all the donkey work and, besides that I, personally, am still, even now, concerned with negotiating with known terrorists. We did that once before, prior to the formation of Israel and that country has been the centre of Middle Eastern conflict ever since, and will probably continue to be so into the future.

At this time I got so angry with politicians in general that in the run up to the general election of 2005 I actually travelled down to London by train with a front-and-back sandwich board that tried to persuade people not to vote at all in the forthcoming election. I walked around the Houses of Parliament three times before returning home; a pretty useless gesture but it vented my wrath somewhat. However, to demonstrate my anger at the time I am reproducing here a load of stuff that was on an old computer; stuff that never saw the light of day...hold tight...here we go:

Yet Another Grumpy Old Man

I am a sixty-one year old pensioner with serious and uncontrollable ...er...er...angst! Yes, angst is definitely the word that feels right to describe my feelings, so I suppose I better look it up to find out what the word actually means! Angst according to my dictionary is "a general feeling of anxiety produced by uncertainties and paradoxes inherent in the state of being human". Yes, that seems to be it alright, particularly the "paradoxes" bit, that definitely seems the word that fits; but to be absolutely sure I better look up the word "paradox" as well. Paradox means "something that is contrary to received conventional opinion; something which is apparently absurd but is or may be really true"...Oh how right that feels!

I live on a planet where the words "democracy", "freedom", and "the rights of the individual" are continually being shoved down my throat at every possible opportunity by those people controlling and influencing my life and "contrary to conventional opinion" I am finding it difficult to believe any of this BOLLOCKS ("n. sing. (slang) nonsense, a muddle, mess").

The particular group of people that seem to use the words "democracy" and "freedom" most frequently are politicians, a group of people with quite a vested interest in perpetuating the use of these words. By using these words as often as they can, they play to the fears of the general public of there being no "democracy" and no "freedom" and in doing so continue to feed their own egos and, of course, their bank balance as well! "Paradoxically", unlike many of the general public, the vast majority of politicians today have never had to defend, in any meaningful way, either "democracy" or "freedom".

One of the more interesting definitions of "democracy" in the dictionary is "a state of society characterized by equality of rights and PRIVELEGES for ALL people". (Help I'm getting that "paradoxy" feeling again!) So, hopefully, when Mr Blair, Mr Cameron or Mr Campbell swan-off to their summer retreats they may consider taking me along with them! But wait, perhaps I am being a bit "parochial" here, and not looking at the bigger picture and not looking to the leading light of "democracy", namely the UNITED STATES of AMERICA; a country to which, despite OUR own long history in matters legal, dating back 1000 years, we scurry off to in order to get legal advice, on blowing people up. Yes, our top legal man, the Attorney General no less, goes off to get legal advice from a country that just over 100 years ago committed mass genocide on a section of its own population by butchering, almost in its entirety, another animal species that that population depended upon for its very existence. Yep, the good old U.S. OF A.; the only country ever to use nuclear weapons against another country, the good old U.S. OF A. where a jury can watch white policemen knock seven shades of S-H-I-T out of some black guy and then find them not guilty, the good old U.S. Of A. where if you are rich and famous you can, apparently, get away with murder! Incidentally, as I'm sure you probably already know, a country that has the right to bear arms by its citizens written into its founding constitution. Yes, a country that is prepared to defend ITS patch (and, of course, any adjoining territories) at any price, including a nuclear holocaust. A country that will invade any other country to protect the extravagant lifestyle of its own people, a country that openly disregards international law ...oh please stop me... stop me ...I'm going on again!

"Democracy" is that ideology that down the years millions have been encouraged by politicians to die for ...without, of course, (and I repeat, unashamedly) the politicians actually getting involved in the dying business themselves! "Democracy" an ideology that has delivered, precisely what? Do I see "all" members of the general public of the democratic countries of this planet free from fear, poverty, exploitation and enjoying the "privileges" of, shall we say politicians...I think not! Yet these democracies insist on exporting their doctrine to all and sundry (sometimes whether they like it or not). Democratic countries are in reality consumer countries; it is nothing to do with any lofty ideals of "democracy", it is more to do with the disgusting business of consumerism, and as the consumables exhaust so too will any pretence of these countries being vaguely democratic. "Democracy" as it is today is a failing experiment, and when the goodies run out so too will the "special relationships", the "ententes cordiale" and all the other "reciprocities" between nations!

Now, "freedom" there's a word! Another word that means different things to different people, that's why politicians love this word so much. Probably more people have died, at the behest of politicians, defending their "freedom" than their "democracy"; and I reckon that most soldiers died in both World Wars believing they were doing so to protect themselves and their families from "foreign" domination and influence; goodness me if they only knew how much of their descendants' lives have now become influenced by dominant "foreigners".

Yes, "freedom" a word worth dying for ...or is it, in fact, a word that is killing us all?! One of the definitions of "freedom" is liberty and that in turn is defined as "freedom from constraint, captivity, slavery or tyranny; freedom to do as one pleases; the unrestrained enjoyment of natural rights; power of free choice etc. etc." Well, I'm having another "paradoxy" feeling again! "Contrary to received, conventional opinion" I do not believe in all this CRAP (n. rubbish) either. We, neither collectively nor individually, should have the freedom to do as we please or be free from constraint, if that particular freedom puts at risk the survival of others, be they human or any other species. Let us take one particular freedom that the human race enjoys at the moment, namely the freedom to convert into carbon dioxide, materials that have remained undisturbed under our feet for millions of years. This particular freedom, which only the more wealthy amongst us can enjoy, has already cost the lives of countless numbers of people, destroyed habitats polluted coastlines and is in the process of reducing this planet, in all probability, to a wasteland of epic proportions! The freedom to burn fossil fuels indiscriminately is not only not discouraged, it is actively promoted everywhere you look. Politicians, who are merely the lackeys of the petrochemical industries and the car lobbyists, are either too corrupt or just too totally gutless to do anything about this "freedom"; the media and all their rich advertising friends have successfully indoctrinated a sheep-like general public over the years into believing that the ordinary person's life is completely meaningless from a status and functional point of view without the use or ownership of the latest conversion machine; and all the other species on this rock that are having their lives dramatically curtailed, strangely enough, don't seem to have much say in the issue at all!

The human race needs to "grow up" fast if we are to save the planet from what lies before us; get rid of the millstone of religion that hangs around our necks dispense with the meaningless frivolities in life; concentrate on the only issue of importance, namely the reduction of CO_2 emissions, and balance our population to our environment!

Now I know and you know, Mr Editor, that there is no way that this letter is going to be published so I will give you something that you might consider publishing, it was going to be "the Real Cost of Legionella", but no I have decided on this instead.

Yes this is word for word from 2006 and no it did not get published in the paper I sent it to! No surprise there then!

In 2005 I received my golden handshake from the RAF and as a result Pam and I decided to go on a trip to St Petersburg.

Chapter 12

Before I tell you about our journey to St Petersburg in 2005, I have found some stuff which illustrates just how political I had become at this time. As I explained earlier I had gone down to London and protested, in my own way, during the run up to the 2005 General Election...well shortly after this election, in June, there was a deferred by-election for South Staffordshire, and each day for a week prior to that election taking place "I got on my bike"...no moped actually, and travelled the fifty mile round trip to the area involved and distributed and pined up the following notice:

VETO THE VOTE

Why?

Well, I was born in Staffordshire over 60 years ago and during my lifetime I have watched as successive governments have abdicated their responsibilities to govern their people to outside agencies; parliament is now almost completely powerless and is now, quite simply, just a well paid talking-shop. As far as serious decisions are concerned the "tails" really do wag the "dog"!

However, that›s not to say parliament cannot exert its authority when the country is in imminent(?) danger of attack. It can send us to WAR!

But, of course, for this to happen the Prime Minister must take legal advice.

Naturally, he must ask the advice of the Attorney General, yet another highly-paid sinecure, who, despite the backing of our legal tradition and heritage....in the case of Iraq...is forced to go scurrying off to the Americans in order to get his card marked by an obviously more mature and well-informed legal system!

Surely, if our 1000 year-old legal system does need advice, for the sake of balance, why not visit Paris, Moscow and Beijing as well?

CONCLUSION

The truth is that whichever candidate you vote for in this election, chances are that it will have absolutely no effect on your life whatsoever...you will still have your house broken into on a regular basis...you will still walk down litter-strewn streets and country lanes....and on cloudless days you will still look up into a grey-blue sky and inhale those man-made particulate materials!

So, please, let›s make this particular South Staffs. Election a referendum on all politicians and just forget about it completely and get on with our own lives despite politicians.

Ronski.

As you can see I'm so full of angst it hurts.

Anyway, on with the show...

Chapter 13

In the summer of 2005 I got a train down to London in order to get visas for Pam and myself from the Russian embassy. When I arrived outside the embassy there was a long queue of people waiting to get their visas; I joined the queue and after three or four hours' wait it was clear I was never going to get inside, so I had to return to Tamworth empty handed. A week or so later both Pam and I went down to London on the same errand but once again it soon became apparent that it was going to be impossible to get visas by this route, so we were forced, at great expense, to use the services of an agency. Having, eventually, secured the necessary documentation at the end of July, Pam and I embarked on our adventure.

We got a train from Tamworth to Newcastle and then a ferry from there to Bergen in Norway where we spent one night in an apartment, arranged for us by the tourist information office, before the following day proceeding by rail to Oslo. Before we set out on this epic journey, rail passes had been purchased from Scanrail which entitled us to travel unhindered throughout Scandinavia and towards Russia. We arrived in Oslo just two days after leaving Tamworth and spent the night there in a Radisson hotel. The following day we travelled by rail to Stockholm in Sweden where another night was spent in an expensive hotel. From Stockholm we travelled by train and then overnight ferry to Helsinki in Finland. The ferry crossing was quite long and totally sleepless, as any attempt at sleep was punctuated by noise of one form or another, so at 2:30 a.m. we gave up and sloped off to the bar to be entertained by an Abba tribute group. Arriving in Helsinki we arranged, via the tourist information office, for accommodation in a hostel for the following two nights and for a later night when we were due to pass through Helsinki again on our return journey. We had to use a hostel because all the hotels were full as the World Athletics Championships were taking place in Helsinki at that time. We spent a couple of days in the Finnish capital, which we appreciated very much; there was good food, some excellent street bands to listen to and we both enjoyed a general feeling of well-being. At this point it's worth mentioning that I could tell you, if necessary, almost every detail of this expedition (and a future one around France), as Pam has kept meticulous diaries of both journeys, recording almost every moment for posterity, but as interesting as they are to me, you, the reader, may not find them as engrossing!

Anyway, we left Helsinki one Friday morning by train towards Vainikkala, the last railway stop inside Finland before we were to cross the Russian border. There had been a couple of time changes on our journey east so far and here was another one, as we had to change to Russian time, yet another one hour advancement on our watches. At the border itself, you might guess, the Russian guards examined all our documentation thoroughly before letting us continue on our journey. We continued, like we had done throughout the whole of our rail travel so far, through a heavily forested landscape, which allowed you very little opportunity to see any of your surroundings as you went along. When we arrived at St Petersburg station we found our way to the metro and descended into the bowels of the earth, for the platform was, indeed, an unbelievable way down. With my limited knowledge of the Cyrillic alphabet (taught to me all those years ago at RAF North Luffenham) I was able to get to the required metro destination, only to find we were still a considerable distance away from our hotel. We were then forced to get a taxi to complete our journey, and this particular taxi driver, clearly, had scant regard for human life, I recall, quite often aiming his vehicle at any pedestrian that dared to cross his path...the man was a lunatic!

We, eventually, arrived at the Matisov Domik hotel that we had booked into, via the web, and which was to be our base for the next couple of days or so.

Having settled in at this reasonably priced and functional hotel we decided to walk to the Mariinsky Theatre to try and get tickets for that evening's ballet performance. We walked through run-down streets and across dangerous roads to the very attractive Mariinsky, but when we got to the place there was clearly a pretty negative attitude towards us and we could not get any sort of response from the woman at the kiosk...she obviously did not like foreigners! The rest of that day was spent sight-seeing, mostly contrasting the opulence of the churches with the poverty of the surroundings in which they stood. After we returned to the hotel, we enjoyed a good evening meal and night's sleep, followed by an adequate breakfast. On that next day we explained to one of the helpful receptionists, Anna, that we had had difficulty managing to get tickets for the ballet at the Mariinsky, and she said that she would come with us to help get some. The upshot of it all was that we not only learned a lot about Anna's life in Russia but we also got tickets for that night's performance at "local" prices... roughly half the price foreigners normally had to pay...and according to Pam's diary I gave a three months pregnant Anna a $40 tip to be spent on her expected baby...but unknown to Pam, of course, I was fairly used to giving money to young foreign girls!

Anyway, we spent the rest of that day exploring St Petersburg; we walked along wide canals into the city centre and visited the famous and stunning Hermitage. Unfortunately we could not gain entrance as they would only accept roubles and so our US dollars were of little use to us here, unlike at most other places throughout the city. Anna had advised us on other places in the city to visit, and after a wonderful, sunny sight-seeing trip we returned to the hotel for a meal before going out to the Mariinsky for the evening performance there. The interior of the theatre was even more attractive than its exterior; the circular construction was crowned by a huge chandelier high up in the middle of a painted ceiling full of colourful cherubs and our box was illuminated with candle-style lights and looked straight down onto the orchestra and stage. The performance, as you might expect, was pretty faultless and during the two intervals we were mixing with the wealthier of St Petersburg's inhabitants plus quite a lot of foreign visitors. The following day was spent sight-seeing and souvenir-hunting around the city and we returned, unhindered, by train to Finland the next day.

We spent a further night at the hostel in Helsinki we had previously stayed at, before setting off, the following morning, on a train journey north to a town called Kemi. The trip lasted eight hours and the passing scenery consisted mostly of large pine forests and great expanses of water and our aim in going to this northern part of Finland was to find our way to and, eventually, cross the Arctic Circle. At the railway station at Kemi we got a taxi and the female taxi driver recommended the Cumulus hotel as a place to stay...we took her advice. Kemi is in Lapland and the capital is Rovaniemi some sixty miles or so further north and close to the Arctic Circle, so we decided that the following day we would get a train there. Pam recalls in her diary that the evening meal there was probably the best meal we had had during the whole of our adventure so far and caused us to book another night in the hotel prior to us continuing our journey into Sweden in two days' time. The following day we took the train up to Rovaniemi and when we arrived there we decided to walk the six miles or so to the Arctic Circle instead of waiting for the bus. The most amazing thing on our walk was experiencing temperatures well into the twenties and seeing gardens full of flowers and plants you would normally associate with more temperate regions, and there were fields full of wheat, sweetcorn and even sunflowers...it was a real eye-opener. Because, as it transpired later, someone had turned around one of the signposts we ended up way off course, and coming to a dead-end I was forced to knock on the door of a nearby house for assistance. Naturally the young woman who answered the door spoke English (as did most everyone in Scandinavia) and she said that her Hungarian husband would help by driving us to the correct route. In the end she, her husband and their young 20 month year old toddler took us, via a visit to a local library, to the Arctic Circle itself. We took pictures of ourselves next to a line painted on the ground and an associated monument that showed visitors to this area where the Arctic Circle actually was. Of course, Lapland is the home of Father Christmas and the nearby log cabins were full of Christmassy type stuff for sale, and there was a constant medley of piped yuletide music blaring out from large outdoor loudspeakers. On a hot summer's day it all seemed so totally out of place. Anyway, this trip around Santa's village cost us about £70 in assorted gifts, which I suppose did help to boost the local economy during this off-peak period. We got a bus back to Rovaniemi in the early evening, and then a train back to Kemi and our hotel, where we spent our last night there eating heartily following a day with very little food.

The next day we got a bus to Tornio on the Finnish/Swedish border and walked, completely unhindered, into Sweden and the town of Haparanda, where we adjusted our watches to Swedish time, and found we were just in time for the bus to Lulea. The bus, I recall, was a smart double-decker with reclining seats and air-conditioning and arrived in Lulea on time, giving us a few hours to explore this pretty town before we needed to get the overnight train to Stockholm. Unfortunately, according to Pam's diary, the sleeper we required was not covered by our Scanrail pass, so we had to fork out an extra £170 for the privilege of getting our heads down on our journey down south. Did I say get our heads down...you must be joking! The sleeping area was small; it had two bunk beds and a separate basic bathroom and very little else, but this enclosure was not the problem; it was the constant braking and speeding up of the train and its continual rocking and rolling from side to side during its travel that rendered any idea of actual sleep almost impossible.

Once again the train arrived in Stockholm exactly on time and we had about an hour or so to wait before our train to Oslo was due to leave. Our return train journey from Stockholm to Oslo is, as usual, meticulously described by Pam in her diary but, of course, as usual, I personally remember absolutely nothing of that trip. In Oslo we had to organise a stay for two nights, which we did by the usual method of using the local tourist information office, and having done that we spent the rest of that day and the following day sight-seeing around the city. The thing about almost everywhere in Scandinavia is its complete lack of litter and Oslo was no exception to that rule; the tidy streets were the thing I most remember and even the inevitable graffiti around the railway stations was done in a more tasteful and artistic way than in the UK. After two days in Oslo we journeyed on to Stavanger which we, of course, did by train; however, according to Pam, we upgraded our seats to "Komfort Class" which entitled us to better seating and free tea and coffee...again I remember absolutely nothing of this.

In Stavanger, where we were due to get our ferry back to the UK from, we booked into a First Hotel, but it proved to be not up to the standard of the one in Oslo...so much so that Pam says, in her diary, that I had considered writing a letter of complaint to the owners...it must have been really poor. After an average evening meal, a night's sleep and a below par breakfast we decided to get a taxi back into town from this rather distant hotel and leave our luggage in the railway station's left luggage lockers so that we could spend the rest of that day luggage-free to explore the city. The first thing we did was to go on a boat trip up one of the nearby fjords; it lasted nearly four hours and you had to be impressed by the sheer steepness and height of the surrounding rockfaces, and a waterfall that cascaded down from a height of nearly six hundred metres. The rest of the day was spent wandering through parkland, recreation grounds and even a cemetery in which were buried the remains of RAF personnel from the Second World War. We also did our share of souvenir buying and spent the last of our money on beer in an Irish pub. Our ferry back to Newcastle was due to leave at midnight so at about 8pm we decided to go and collect our luggage from the station. What panic ensued when we discovered that the left-luggage section of the station closed at 6pm on a Saturday night and would not open until the following morning... Help! We rushed around like demented loonies asking anyone and everyone that spoke even a little English what we could do to retrieve our baggage. We eventually found a door with an intercom and a voice at the other end told us that it would cost us about £30 to get a security guard out to enter the left-luggage section and retrieve our items...but we had no money left as I explained to the guy at the other end of the intercom. Anyway this gentleman eventually came to the door and, clearly seeing our distressed state, took pity and our locker keys and entered the enclosed left-luggage section to retrieve our luggage for us...what a guy! We then proceeded to the nearby ferry waiting area where we could recover from the trauma of it all and eat the last of our rations.

The ferry journey back to Newcastle was fairly uneventful, apart from the fact that I saw a whale, and when we arrived back in the UK we were greeted by an aggressive drunk and streets full of litter...welcome home!

Chapter 14

Further to our trip to St Petersburg here is a letter that was written to our local newspaper shortly after we returned from our holiday; whether it was printed or not I cannot recall (but I doubt it).

Since neither my partner nor I wish to get embroiled in what the rest of you are doing to the planet, we choose not to own a car and never fly abroad for our annual holiday. We cycle or walk to work and use public transport for all other journeys. We are both in our early sixties and up until this year have always holidayed together in this country. However, this year I became eligible for an RAF pension and as a result decided to treat my partner and myself to a holiday abroad.

After considering many options we decided to tour Scandinavia by train after ferrying from Newcastle to Norway. The journey would take us through Norway, Sweden and Finland to our furthest point St Petersburg in Russia. On the return journey we would also visit the Arctic Circle in northern Finland.

Well I am sure your readers will be pleased to know that we executed our plans perfectly and had the most wonderful time; however, your readers may not wish to know the following:

We visited and stayed in Bergen, Oslo, Stockholm, Helsinki, St Petersburg, Kemi, Rovaniemi, Lulea and finally Stavanger and in the process passed through numerous other towns and villages and in all that time I can honestly say that I could not have filled one black plastic bag with litter from all those streets we walked through!

This country is quite simply...DISGUSTING.

Also during our travels we walked past many thousands of people, many of them teenagers, and I never felt at all threatened! Whereas here I only have to go down the road for a newspaper and there's a load of youngsters just "looking for it".

I am sorry but litter on our streets is just a symptom of some deeper underlying problems we have with our youngsters for it is they that are predominantly the offenders when it comes to dropping litter.

Never mind the three "Rs"; all children from the earliest of ages must be taught to put things away after use, leave as you find or clear up afterwards! This discipline can only aid in clarity of thought in later years.

Yours sincerely,

Well that gives some idea of my strength of feeling at that time and which, for the most part, is a feeling that remains with me to this day…and if the reader (if he/she is still out there) will indulge me a little further I will give you some more vitriol I spewed out at about this time:

As far as my mental health is concerned, I have to admit that I am in need of the most rigorous psychiatric help! My spondylitis, hiatus hernia and diverticulitis have clearly had an effect on my mental well-being over the last few years, you see I actually believe that 99% of the people I meet on a day-to-day basis are in fact alien creatures intent on destroying the planet! I know these are fanciful delusions but if you will allow me, I will tell you why I think my beliefs are well-founded.

These creatures that surround me everywhere are, I believe, part of a world-wide network; some of whom draw off large quantities of liquid from under the ground and pass it around the world to their fellow aliens. They then, almost as one, proceed to convert this liquid in their wretched machines into toxic gases that they release into the atmosphere! Some of these disgusting creatures actually seem to get pleasure from this process, even though they must surely know it will eventually kill their own offspring and, even worse, destroy for ever thousands of other species of life that have taken over 3,000 million years to evolve into their present state!

When you meet these aliens socially or at work they actually boast to one another about the size and newness of their conversion machines and about how they have travelled halfway around the world and back in even bigger super converting machines!

Their whole lives revolve around these machines in one way or another and they actively educate and encourage their offspring to pursue a similar lifestyle to their own.

If you engage these creatures in logical conversation and suggest maybe they should perhaps try and curb their planet-destroying antics, they immediately go into a maniacal rage. They thrash about in denial, their tentacles waving around in all directions. They usually make the same lame excuses for their lifestyle:

1. Any financial curb on their "evil" practices by real humans would clearly be a case of victimising the "poor motorist", while the rich among them could continue enjoying themselves.
2. The next excuse is to deny, schoolboy-like, that they are doing anything alien at all ...The climate has, after all, always varied over geological time... "Nothing to do with us, guv'nor."
3. Finally, many of them go into mumbo-jumbo talk and tell you of the great alien being in the sky they call GOD who is controlling all our destinies and how they are just part of His divine plan!

Yes these creatures are incapable of objective thought and they are spreading everywhere; they are spreading across the globe even unto India and China. They are quite simply "evil" and need to be stopped NOW! Obviously with all these absurd thoughts in my mind there must be something terribly wrong with my mental state.

All this was written in response to a request I made, at that time, for Incapacity Benefit (on the advice from my local unemployment office), a request which was totally rejected by the powers that be.

It was about this time, and for the next few years, that I became seriously involved in trying to prevent our local council giving permission for a housing development to be built on the banks of the Anchor river, and later on in other areas around Tamworth including our municipal golf course.

I wrote numerous letters to the Tamworth Herald on the subject and attended several council meetings to explain that I thought these developments would increase the flood risk to Tamworth and the surrounding areas, and would, inevitably, destroy dwindling wildlife habitats. I handed out leaflets in the town and protested with my placards outside the council offices, but of course, in the end, 10 years on, it all proved a totally useless exercise and the bulldozers and earthmovers moved in...but they will pay the price eventually, I suspect!

Chapter 15

In 2007 Pam retired and we decided to go on a holiday trip around France. We acquired a rail pass that allowed us to travel on eight rail trips within one month throughout France and we made our way to Poole in Dorset where we would get our cross-channel ferry. We arrived in St Malo at about 7:30 p.m. and I decided that a taxi was not required to take us to the "nearby" hotel we had organised on the web days before. Instead I chose to drag our large suitcase and carry a heavy backpack to the hotel using a recently acquired map of St Malo. Of course, I managed to get totally lost and spent the next two and a half hours alongside a heavily laden Pam "touring" the suburbs of the town before eventually having to resort to a taxi to get us to the hotel... which, unfortunately, turned out to be pretty basic. We spent a couple of days in St Malo sightseeing before starting our trip into the interior of the country. We decided initially to go to Nantes, a journey that took us through Rennes, but when we arrived at Nantes the outlook from that station looked a bit industrialised, so noticing there was a train to La Rochelle due to depart we hopped on that instead. At La Rochelle we found the "Office de Tourisme" and through them booked a four-night stay in a nearby hotel. Another fairly basic hotel but it did have an indoor swimming pool which we took immediate advantage of...of course, all this (and the remainder of our trip) is remembered through another of Pam's well-kept diaries...the only fault I can find with her detailed diaries is that she gives precise accounts of practically every meal that we ever had during the whole of this trip and it was the same, I have to say, with our Scandinavian holiday of two years earlier.

Anyway, we both liked La Rochelle very much and there was a very colourful trans-Atlantic yacht race about to start from the marina there that very weekend and that, along with a visit to a very large and wonderful aquarium, gave us plenty to occupy our time in La Rochelle. Unfortunately, Pam was suffering very badly with a bad back and there was some doubt about us continuing the holiday so we decided to get the train back up to Paris in case we needed to "bail out" to St Malo for a return journey back to England. By the time we got to Paris Pam was feeling a bit better and after a night in a hotel near to the Montparnasse station and close to a sixty storey high "monolith" of a building, the following day we "did" Paris by metro, visiting all the usual tourist traps.

After our one night in Paris we travelled down to Clermont Ferrand on the edge of the Massif Central, a highland region in the middle of southern France, where we spent one night in a hotel close to the railway station. The town itself was rather larger than expected, and because of a lot of different conferences going on in the town at the time we were advised by the tourist information office that if we wished to stay in the area we would be better off trying to find accommodation in the smaller nearby town of Riom. Now the French, admirably, do like their dogs but they do not appear to like clearing up after them, so everywhere we went in France we always had to be careful not to tread in any dog crap...it wasn't like that in Scandinavia!

In Riom our basic accommodation was the bottom floor of a 16th century tower and there was a spiral staircase leading to the two sets of accommodation above us. Riom didn't offer much to the tourist so the local advice was to go to Pontgibaud with its surrounding ancient volcanic landscapes. The journey by rail to Pontgibaud was described by Pam as being "brilliant" as it climbed through a landscape full of greenery and lovely views with the occasional bird of prey sitting atop the taller of the many trees. The railway station at Pontgibaud was well outside the town and we were forced into a twenty-minute walk through delightful countryside before actually getting into the town itself. It was a pretty town where we indulged ourselves in assorted and inexpensive appetizing snacks and drinks, which we consumed on a picnic table adjacent to a sun-drenched and gently flowing river. We tried to gain access to a local historic landmark, that of Chateau-Dauphin, but unfortunately it was closed, so we had to admire this medieval castle from afar. Luckily the first part of our return journey to Riom was to be by bus to Clermont Ferrand and this started from the town of Pontgibaud itself so no long walks back to the train station were involved. We spent the four hours or so before the bus arrived sitting outside a nearby hotel drinking copious amounts of the local beer and getting pleasantly intoxicated. The bus arrived on time and we got back to Riom safely enough, in time for an evening meal and a carafe of local red wine...now totally pissed and ready for sleep.

The following sunny day we travelled on foot to the nearby Chatel-Guyon along a main road that had no pavement, so we were forced to face the oncoming traffic in the cycle lane and we just hoped for the best. The walk along this quite busy road was through a scenic countryside and led us into a most picturesque little town. There was a "thermal park" there where loads of OAPs were sitting around in the sun drinking the free mineral water issuing from a nearby fountain. The water tasted "soapy" to Pam but I could only taste and smell its sulphurous content, akin to the smell of bad eggs...however, it was drunk by many mainly elderly people because of its high mineral content and in the belief that it was good for you...who knows? Indeed there was a promotional video displayed on a large television screen in the area that showed a woman purported to be 113 years old who had benefited from the lifelong use of this spring water...who knows?

A missed bus caused us to hang around in the town a bit longer than intended and the bus we did eventually catch was full of noisy schoolkids returning home. We passed a chemist's on the journey back that had an illuminated sign displaying, amongst other things, the current temperature...so on the 21st September at roughly 5 p.m. it showed a temperature of 32 degrees Celsius ...a portent of what was and is to come in later years!

Back in Riom we showered and changed before going out for a rather expensive meal at a nearby restaurant and after one more night in our tower we set off to our next destination which was to be Toulouse. Our journey to Toulouse took us, initially, along a single track line that clung to the sides of steep sided valleys...very picturesque but a bit scary! We stopped briefly at Aurillac, described by Pam as a "sprawling any-town", before continuing on to Toulouse. We travelled through more pleasing-to-the-eye countryside, full of lots of wide rivers and endless fields of sweetcorn that eventually transformed, later in our travel, into numerous large vineyards.

Toulouse, on arrival, was overcast and very humid. We made our way out of the station and over a bridge and soon spotted a pleasant looking hotel, so we decided to give it a go. The manager spoke reasonable English, telling us that there were rooms available, and so we decided to book in for a three-night stay. The hotel had a really interesting internal configuration in that there was a central rectangular atrium crowned by a glass roof around which balconies ran on four levels and from which all the hotel rooms were attached...almost prison-like. The benefit of the glass roof was that numerous potted plants and much greenery could be grown, giving the inside of the hotel an airy outdoor feel...I liked it. Our room was small but functional and had an en-suite facility with plenty of towels, soaps and shampoos and there were "welcoming" sweets on our pillows...Pam writes: "luxury indeed!".

An evening meal at a nearby cafe went down well especially with the cheap, but very acceptable, local red and we were entertained on our way back to the hotel, in one square, by a carnival group dancing and playing drums ...all very festive. The following morning there was a threat of rain and so on the way out of the hotel the kind manager rushed after us to give us an umbrella in case it did rain ...but the cynic in me notices that the hotel name is emblazoned all over it...how mean-spirited can I get! That day was spent exploring the city, including walking along the towpaths of wide canals, a visit to a "super" food market and a boat trip down the river Garonne. On our second day based in Toulouse we decided to take a train to Carcassonne; unfortunately the train did not leave on time for some inexplicable reason, the patient passengers having to wait two hours on board a stationary train, so we did not arrive in Carcassonne until 1 p.m. Of course, all this stuff is coming from Pam's diary, but even I can remember how hot it was for a late September day when we arrived at our destination. From the station, which was adjacent to the Canal du Midi, we crossed over an old bridge and walked up the hill to the sun drenched medieval part of the town. This castle on a hill was full of cobbled streets, high stone walls, ramparts and stone parapets and had been the ideal location for many a medieval play or film. Down in the main part of Carcassonne we fed ourselves and spent the rest of our time in the place watching narrowboats negotiating their way through one of the locks on the canal.

Back in Toulouse, since it was our last night there, we found our way, eventually, to a rather expensive restaurant and took advantage of some of their excellent cuisine whilst deciding definitely that Avignon was to be our next "port of call". The train to Avignon was again half an hour late leaving the station; this country is so unlike Scandinavia when it comes to the punctuality of their trains. The train journey was on an old fashioned type train with separate compartments and we had to share ours with three New Zealanders here for the

Rugby World Cup, a French lady and a German Lufthansa airline pilot. Pam's diary is full of our conversations with these people, the most interesting of whom was the verbose polymath, the pilot. I will not bother with the details here except to say that we all agreed that Bush was a tosser. Anyway, our fellow travellers all got off at Beziers and were replaced by a guitar-playing young man and his girlfriend.

We arrived at Avignon at 4 p.m. and settled into a poor quality, but relatively cheap, hotel down a side street that overlooked a church statue and a tower that lit up at night. Pam's diary tells me that I found the room key to the hotel room in Toulouse in my pocket so we had to spend time finding a post office, with the obvious stretching of our knowledge of the French language, to ensure its safe return. After food and wine under the umbrellas of a cafe in the Place de l'Horloge we retired to our bed in the attic at the quite early time of 9:30 p.m. The following morning we ate a surprisingly good breakfast at the hotel and were re-allocated to a small en-suite room saving us from having to negotiate a dangerous spiral staircase in the middle of the night to have a pee.

Strange how one 15th century French folk song about a dance on (actually under) a half-completed bridge can generate a vast tourist industry attracting visitors from all over the world. Anyway, after breakfast we found our way to an elevated park area that gave us an excellent view over the town and the famous Avignon bridge; a bridge, by the way, where you have to spend good money for the dubious pleasure of just standing on it...we did not indulge at this time. Neither did we spend money visiting an old Papal palace where a number of popes resided during the 14th century when they got their knickers in a twist over an edict by the crown that they should move to Rome... organised religion!...what a waste of space! Instead, we caught a FREE ferry to an island in the middle of the river Rhone where we strolled around orchards full of pears and apples and drank more red wine on a cafe terrace whilst enjoying the sunny view back across the river to the Pope's palace and the Avignon bridge. The remaining couple of cooler days in Avignon were spent sight-seeing and buying the odd gift including a small pottery cicada that chirps when you pass it... it's still in our hallway to this day. We also witnessed a protest strike by taxi drivers, had a meeting with some scally Liverpool supporting tourists (much to Pam's delight) and were even tempted into stepping onto the Pont d'Avignon.

Our visit to Avignon ended with a decision to move on to Annecy, a place recommended by the "lost" children that Pam had, only a few years earlier, been reunited with. We passed through Valence on our way to Annecy and experienced more wonderful scenery enroute, arriving at our cool destination that enjoyed the "freezing cold" temperature of 9 degrees C. Via the Office de Tourisme we found our way to a 3 star hotel whose room did, at least, have a TV and an en-suite. After a brief poke around the place we set off to have a look around the very wet town and, since it was raining so heavily, we purchased a large umbrella from a nearby store. Even in the rain and dwindling light we could see it was a pretty place with its cobbled streets, neat little bridges over its river and canal and with plenty of flower-filled hanging baskets liberally sprinkled throughout. The following sunny day we walked along the banks of Lake Annecy admiring the beautiful views of snow-capped mountains and noticing the purity and clarity of the lake water. We took a boat trip on one of the cleanest lakes in Europe, according to our boat's guide, and we noticed how many little villages there were dotted around the edge of the lake behind each of which were picturesque conifer-filled slopes leading up to those snow-capped Alpine mountains...are they snow-capped anymore?...I doubt it...if they are, they certainly won't be in a few years' time! We spent a further two days in Annecy doing lots of touristy stuff and regretted leaving this most pleasant of areas of

France, but we really did need to start on our way back north and west towards St Malo and our ferry back to the UK.

Our next stop was to be Dijon and we had to go via Lyon, a journey that took us through an enormous tunnel around part of the even more enormous Lake Bourget near Aix de Bains. All the intercity trains in France travel at terrifyingly fast speeds but even on one of these fast trains it still, according to Pam, took between 10 and 15 minutes to pass the lake in its entirety. When we got to Lyon we had about two hours to spare before our train to Dijon left, so we sat in a cafe outside the station with a beer watching the world go peacefully by but, unfortunately, later on we were interrupted by a number of rowdy kilted Scotsmen there to watch the Rangers match against Lyon that evening. The journey up to Dijon from Lyon took just over two hours and passed through a more flatter terrain full of yet more sweetcorn and with trees that had now started to get a more autumnal tinge to their leaves. At Dijon the tourist information office was close to the station and all the hotel accommodation in the city centre that they advised was totally out of our price-range, but we were also told that if we travelled further out from the centre there were much cheaper places. We fixed up with them a stay in a small hotel in a place called Chevigny, about seven miles outside Dijon, and were given a map and directions for the bus journey there. On leaving the tourist information office we were caught in an almighty thunderstorm and soaking wet and with a load of wet luggage we arrived, after a big unscheduled detour and a bus full of screaming schoolchildren, at our destination. It proved to be a very basic accommodation, hardly a hotel as its name implied, more like a B&B; the additional rooms to our sleeping area appeared to be just a busy and smoky pub/bar with connected eating area alongside, where we assumed we would be served our breakfast in the mornings that followed...it all felt very French. On the following misty morning we bussed back into Dijon and then out to a local attraction called Toison d'Or (Golden Fleece) having been given the impression it was a delightful park area, but Pam's description probably summed it up correctly as being "an assault course, a pond and a few flower beds"; it transpired that its real claim to fame was as a huge glamorous shopping complex, the name of which in English proved to be oh so totally apt! We quickly returned into a sunnier Dijon and spent time sight-seeing around the city before returning to our "hotel" in Chevigny. It proved to be a disappointing evening for Pam as we watched Liverpool lose 1-0 at home against Marseille on French TV.

The next day we set off back into Dijon to check out the following day's train times to Tours and to have a look around the old town part of the city and had a peaceful bite to eat in the Botanical Gardens.

The next day we said farewell to Dijon, a place Pam regarded as a bit "soulless", and travelled on to Paris where, thanks to my good self, we managed to, unnecessarily, zig zag across the city to catch a slow train from Austerlitz station to Tours.

The initial impression of Tours was that it looked "a right old dump" but that impression proved far from the truth and a helpful Tourist Office close to the station fixed us up with a 2 star hotel in a little nearby tree-lined square. The room at the hotel was excellent for the money; it was on the first floor, was light and airy with a high ceiling and had French windows that opened out onto the square below. It was market day in the square so we indulged in some of the locally made quiches but certainly not the ones involving escargot. Despite the very pleasant hotel room it soon became clear why this hotel was only 2 star as we did not get any sleep until 5 a.m. because of the disco noise coming from a nearby nightclub. At breakfast in the morning an English couple who were staying there said that they were going to leave because of the disco noise but we said we would give it another night hoping that the disco was just one of those Friday night things.

During that sunny day we strolled around the old town; it was full of timbered buildings and, of course, numerous tourist-grabbing cafes. We visited a museum in an old medieval building, had a main meal at Cafe Gerrard (Liverpool supporting Pam's choice) and enjoyed a peaceful trip in a wooden boat on the River Loire. Back at the hotel that whole night was punctuated by more intrusive disco noise along with a cacophony of car horns blaring continually because France had managed to beat New Zealand at rugby... We, regretfully, surrendered and chose to spend our remaining couple of nights back in St Malo. We travelled back to St Malo and a hotel there organized for us by a kind ticket assistant at Tours station, and travelled to the port via Paris and Rennes; the journeys to Paris and then onto Rennes were both on those terrifyingly fast French intercity trains but the local train from Rennes to St Malo was on a slower, but equally as scary, rickety old train that rumbled and groaned its way along in a totally unstable manner.

Unlike before in St Malo we chose a taxi to our outlying hotel ...certainly no walking! ...and were taken to a fairly standard establishment that at least gave us a good quiet night's sleep. After a satisfactory breakfast the following morning we chilled out with a long slow walk through coastal parkland, an area full of large old expensive-looking houses and then on towards a busy seaside promenade where we ate our lunch before a relaxing walk along the beach into the centre of town itself. A bus trip back to our hotel followed by a meal in our room that we had bought from a nearby supermarket and another early night ended our day.

Our last day in France and there was a threat of rain and all attempts we made to arrange for a hotel in Weymouth, where our ferry was due to dock, failed so we decided to taxi into St Malo and leave our disintegrating luggage in the railway station's left luggage until nearer to our ferry time. When we got to the station there was no left luggage department so we were forced to haul our dying luggage in the pouring rain around the town looking for an internet cafe. We eventually found one and managed to book one night in the Sun Inn in Weymouth for £75...the most expensive booking we had made throughout the whole of our adventure. Our large case with most of our luggage in had now got almost impossible to drag because the wheels had worn down completely and the body of the case was dragging on the floor, particularly over the many cobbled areas of St Malo, so we decided to head for the ferry terminal rest area even though there was still six hours before the ferry. When we arrived there, soaking wet, we fed on accumulated snacks and waited for the ferry time to arrive. Luckily at around 2 p.m. the ferry people allowed us to check in, a full four hours before the ferry was due to depart, so we were able to dump our luggage on the conveyor belt and forget about it until Weymouth. We went back into old St Malo town and found a bowl with the name Emile on it, something Pam had been looking for, in vain, throughout the whole of our trip around France; it was for her first, recently arrived, grandchild. In order to celebrate this monumental event (the bowl and the grandchild) we went into a nearby cafe and got through a whole bottle of fairly expensive red... in the middle of the afternoon...outrageous! After a choppy crossing across the Channel via Jersey and Guernsey we arrived in Weymouth about midnight and the manager of the Sun Inn had waited up for us, but the room was total crap. It was up three flights of stairs, had a communal toilet across the corridor opposite, the double bed had no bedside table or lighting, there was a poxy little shower and wash basin in the corner of the room with a broken towel rail and there was intrusive street lighting outside the window...what a shithole for £75 per night!...welcome back to the UK. In the morning we got a train back to Poole and from there a couple of trains back to Tamworth... and so ended our French adventure.

Chapter 16

MORE VITRIOL AND AN AMAZING REVELATION

Back in dear old Blighty I continued my single-man onslaught against our local planning department and their plans for more housing development along the banks of the river Anchor, and other green places, by more protests and letters to the Tamworth Herald. But about this time I also "vented my spleen" against others. After watching an edition of the Weather Show on the BBC I wrote this letter to them:

The BBC Weather (Disinformation) Show

Well could you ever have believed that a programme like the BBC Weather Show could be used as a vehicle for disinformation? Smiley, smiley Carol Kirkwood fronts a programme full of her smiley, smiley weather presenters oozing reassurances over the effects of global warming. We are shown a simplistic map of the globe with two white blobs at the top and bottom to represent the north and south poles and are told by the smiling presenter about what the effect of the melting of these two areas might have on sea levels. Reassuringly the presenter had spent two and a half years under Antarctic ice, so we are all supposed to be happy he knows what he is talking about! He then goes on to tell us about the effects of the melting Arctic icecap; in which he compares this monumental event with the mundane occurrence of a cube of ice melting in a glass of water. He tells us that because this icecap does not cover any land mass it will hardly affect world sea levels. What he failed to discuss is the bloody great land mass of Greenland (conveniently NOT coloured white) next to the Arctic icecap with its huge area of rapidly melting mountains of ice!

He continues by discussing the effects that a melting Antarctic might have on sea-levels; telling us about how this ice sheet only covers a "few islands" as though the land mass under the Antarctic was of little significant size, and finally concludes the whole business by implying that global warming effects are two or three hundred years down the line anyway ...so no worries then!

The programme continues with the ever smiling Carol Kirkwood having a jolly good time around the aviation industry. (What a girl she is! How reassuring it is to know that this knowledgeable professional has no hang ups at all about air travel and its contribution to global warming.)

I could hardly supress my seething anger by the time two other smiley, smiley weathermen tell us the Institute of Hydrology and whoever have (fortunately) come to the conclusion that last year's flooding was not caused by global warming at all, but was just a freak event; presumably similar in its freakishness to the one that occurred at Boscastle only a couple of years earlier!

And those Carol Kirkwood outtakes at the end of the programme defy description; I was really rolling out of my chair by then.

Once upon a time the BBC was an impartial observer and reporter of world events; clearly, like a stable climate, those days are long gone!

Yours sincerely

I even tried my hand at a bit of poetry to express my feelings:

The Insanity Of Humanity

Daily, The Media moulds the young vulnerable brains,
With yet more and more anthropocentric refrains,
While the planet simply complains and complains,
About the avalanche of cars, trucks and planes.

Politicians promise the Earth,
Without knowing the Earth,
While other species fail to rebirth,
Amidst human laughter, satire and mirth.

Religious leaders promise eternal life,
Through the rubble and the strife,
Parasitically plunging a twisted blade,
Into the heart that reason made.

Planners concrete over...for financial gain,
The green that absorbs the heavier rain,
Runoff swells the swollen main,
And homes (and the sea) become a cesspit's drain.

The "Privileged" press for continual growing,
To keep their oily black finances flowing,
Polar caps retreat from snowing and snowing,
And white bears' hearts start slowing and slowing.

Those myopic advocates of continual growth,
Care nothing for child and grandchild both,
Care nothing for all of nature that feeds us,
And should go to hell or more appropriately the US...eh!

Yes, there was more but the reader (if there is one) needs to conclude with the final irony of it all...

Chapter 17

In July 2008 Pam and I were working in the back garden and I thought I heard the postman push something through the front door. It was a hot day and I remember taking the letter that had come through the letterbox into the garden to read it. The letter was from our local newspaper that wanted my permission to release my address to a woman in Cornwall who claimed to be my DAUGHTER...This was almost forty years ago to the day that I married my first wife Joyce; could this woman actually be the product of that brief relationship? My brain EXPLODED...how did this woman in Cornwall get hold of my name? If she was indeed my daughter what did she look like?... and what did she do?...and how had she come to be living in Cornwall? Thousands of questions needed to be answered so, of course, I gave my permission to the newspaper for the release of my address. Within days I received a letter from the woman that convinced me that she was indeed my daughter. The woman in Cornwall had apparently found my name via her aunt Marg and her remote contact with Paul X (remember him?), who had been living in Burton on Trent and had picked up, by chance, a copy of the Tamworth Herald in which my name had appeared in connection with my protests against the local planners. Her name was J and she had moved to Cornwall with her family when she was nine. She had gone through a bad time recently in which she had lost twins in late pregnancy and also lost her beloved dog. She had apparently been looking for me for much of her adult life, ever since her mother Joyce had thrown her birth certificate at her in an argument on her eighteenth birthday and told her that the man she thought was her father was not her real dad and she was in fact the daughter of the guy named on the birth certificate. She had three brothers that now suddenly became stepbrothers and a father that now suddenly became a stepfather and, so, I was told, she walked out and went to live with her nan (my ex-mother-in-law) and Marg. The letters she wrote to me were littered with spelling errors, so clearly she was no academic ...but she was MY DAUGHTER!...and what sort of a shit am I for noticing that! My heart was full of sympathy for her with her recent losses and her difficult earlier years. A meeting was soon arranged for myself and Pam to go down to Cornwall to meet her, and I met my daughter for the first time on Truro railway station. I knew immediately she was my daughter as she was the spitting image of my sister's daughter Al. My new and only offspring drove us back to her home ...and what a home! It was a large detached old miner's cottage in the middle of nowhere with four acres of land, a huge conservatory, outdoor swimming pool and with a nearby recently built "granny flat" where J's mother-in-law lived. Of course, being my daughter, she had a new dog, an affectionate springer spaniel, a cat and a rabbit in a hutch outside. In this cottage I noticed a large brown porcelain horse (with a broken leg)...a prize that I had once won in a race forty years earlier!

Now, here we get to the painfully hard bit for me, her husband S was a **car salesman** who was out at work in a distant showroom that he had to get to with the aid of their second car. Indeed J's mother-in-law A was in possession of two vehicles...I contented myself with the fact that cars were essential in such a remote part of Cornwall, but found it very hard to stomach that they flew on regular holidays abroad away from such an idyllic environment...but she was MY DAUGHTER. Her husband S was a workaholic who worked long hours and when at home spent nearly all of his time tending and landscaping the four acres that surrounded his home. He probably felt he needed regular holidays abroad to relieve the stresses of his very demanding job. After a few more meetings both in Cornwall and Tamworth my daughter and her husband S became aware of my "green" leanings, but to this day I have never let her know just how strong my "green" feelings are. Anyway, whether it was the stabilizing effect of my introduction into her life, as some have suggested, or not, she soon gave birth to two sons. I have two grandsons F. and H. to go with Pam's eight grandchildren, two from each of her children.

Since that time over ten years ago time has rushed by, as it tends to do in old age, and during the intervening period I have lost both of my remaining siblings, have inherited, and eventually lost, from Pam's youngest daughter a most wonderful staffy bitch...a loss that I still cannot come to terms with, watched the growing up of ten grandchildren, had two pulmonary embolisms, lost loads of cash in our local betting shop and continued to secretly write stuff to highlight my feelings on topics of the day.

This book has been about my somewhat reckless early life and a more embittered (just like my father) older time, but I am a fault finder by nature...it's what I do! However, I will leave you on some more positive reflections, and those concern our NHS.

My partner, Pam, who is two years older than me, has had the quality of her life considerably improved by a re-surfacing of one hip and the replacement of the other...all courtesy of our NHS.

Pam's daughter Suzi's son was dying after one week of life before Birmingham Children's Hospital intervened with microsurgery on his little heart...he is now a bouncing two year old...courtesy of our NHS.

I, myself, have recently cheated death twice after two P.Es (the last one a touch and go job)...courtesy of our NHS. So, whether you think that this is a good thing or a bad thing, the NHS is directly responsible for enabling me to write this rambling tale and give you, the reader, an insight into one ordinary bloke's life!

THE END

www.ingramcontent.com/pod-product-compliance
Lightning Source LLC
Chambersburg PA
CBHW061332040426
42444CB00011B/2891